THE PUZZLES OF JOB

by

ORD L. MORROW

Associate Radio Minister
Back to the Bible Broadcast

A
BACK TO THE BIBLE
Publication

39¢ each
3 for $1.00
(Quantity prices on request)

order from

BACK TO THE BIBLE BROADCAST
Box 233   Lincoln, Nebr. 68501

FOREWORD

The Book of Job is considered by some scholars to be the oldest book in the world. That alone would make it a significant work. Of even greater importance, however, is its inspired message. It raises questions that thoughtful men and women have pondered in every generation.

Each of Job's puzzles has a Biblical answer. Mr. Morrow thoroughly explores both the questions and the answers. He fully recognizes, however, that a complete answer to some of these puzzles awaits a future day when we shall no longer see through a glass darkly. In the meantime we can rest with confidence in the wisdom and righteousness of God as did Abraham when he concluded a plea to God in these words: "Shall not the Judge of all the earth do right?" (Gen. 18.25).

These messages on Job were delivered over the international radio network of Back to the Bible Broadcast. We are happy to publish them in this form and thereby fulfill the requests of many of our radio friends.

—John I. Paton
Literature Editor

CONTENTS

Chapter One

WHY DO CHRISTIANS SUFFER?

Though written nearly 3500 years ago, the Book of Job is as up-to-date as if it had been written in our day. It is very possible that more persons know of Job than they do of almost any other individual of ancient times. The Book of Job is one we may not understand completely, but much of it comes right home to us because Job deals with the very things that we must live with, think about and find an answer to. These are things from which none of us are exempt, such as sorrow, pain, suffering, change, fear, hope, death and eternity.

Some persons look on this book as being one of pure philosophy because it deals with principles and life experiences to be found in every age. It is much more than that, however, for it is a story of a man who really lived, a man as human as any of us. He was a man who came to grips with things that even today strain the faith of men to the breaking point. This book is a record of a man who laid bare his soul before God and poured out his complaints in words we would all like to call our own at times. Job said, "Therefore I will not refrain my mouth; I will speak in the anguish of my spirit; I will complain in the bitterness of my soul" (7:11).

This is one of the poetic books of the Bible. Its poetic form, however, does not detract for a moment from its inspiration. What better form could one use for expressing the deep things of the inner life? Poetry can often phrase the cries of the soul that prose would never dare to attempt. Just as expressions of love seem fitting and even move us deeply when expressed through poetry, the same thoughts put in the form of prose might leave us unmoved or even provoke us to laughter.

The words of Job were not hasty words. He sat in silence for seven days before taking up the series of conversations with his friends that occupy the bulk of the book. Undoubtedly these debates, for such they were, took a number of days to complete. The ancient sufferer may not have thought through all of his statements completely, but he did think about them.

He was no stoic, suffering in silence. He was a man of deep feeling. We can almost picture him as he sat upon a heap of ashes groaning because of bodily affliction and moaning out his unfathomable grief at the loss of his family and possessions. He made known his desires to God even though he may have questioned whether or not God would hear or that God would care. Is this not the way we sometimes respond to the hard places in life?

This is a supremely human and personal book. Job did not look for answers to settle problems between nations nor for remedies for the world's ills. He was searching for answers to the problems that are common to all of us. He looked for a bridge over the deep chasm that separated him from God. In so doing he became a man who can be identified with every age. We still speak of severe suffering as "suffering like Job," or patience under trial as "the patience of Job."

Little is known of Job outside the book that bears his name except for two other passages in Scripture. In Ezekiel 14:14, the Lord speaks of the righteousness of Job and compares it with that of Noah and Daniel. In the New Testament James says, "Behold, we count them happy which endure. Ye have heard of the patience of Job, and have seen the end of the Lord; that the Lord is very pitiful, and of tender mercy" (5:11).

When first introduced to us, Job is seen as a very prosperous man yet one who was careful to see that his prosperity did not hinder his service for God. The Lord himself testified of this, saying that there was no man like Job in all the earth, a perfect and upright man, one who feared God and shunned evil. Yet calamity befell him. His oxen, asses and camels were stolen, his sheep and servants killed by fire; and all his children died when a violent wind destroyed the house in which they were eating. It was from this background of loss and tragedy that Job faced some of the greatest puzzles of life. And the things that puzzled Job are the very things that puzzle us.

There were at least seven major puzzles for which Job sought a solution, the first one having to do with pain and suffering. It is a subject as old as the human race. Two passages tell us of Job's feeling about this: "Wherefore is light given to him that is in misery, and life unto the bitter in soul; Which long for death, but it cometh not; and dig for it more than for hid treasures; Which rejoice exceedingly, and are glad, when they can find the grave? Why is light given to a man whose way is hid, and whom God hath hedged in? For my sighing cometh before I eat, and my roarings are poured out like the waters" (3:20-24). Then in chapter 7 Job said, "So am I made to possess months of vanity, and wearisome nights are appointed to me. When I lie down, I say, When shall I arise, and the night be gone? and I am full of tossings to and fro unto the dawning of the day. My flesh is clothed with worms and clods of dust; my skin is broken, and become loathsome" (vv. 3-5). Job wondered why he was kept alive. He wanted to know the purpose of the pain and suffering he was enduring. Job found himself

> Weary of hoping hopes that seem vain,
> Weary of struggles—never ending,
> Weary of thinking when nothing seems plain,
> Weary of life—meaningless.

Never once in all of this did Job speak of suicide. He could desire that the Lord would see fit to end his suffering, but he would not end it himself. Suicide is not the solution for life's problems. Despair is a miserable place for anyone to seek refuge, for there is no refuge in it. It is far better to be a living dog in the will of God than to be a dead lion out of it.

There is more than one kind of pain and suffering. Physical suffering is often hard to endure. No one knows how severe this road is except one who has been over it or is in the midst of it. Those of us who have had little physical suffering must sympathize in silence. Only those who know what pain is can share in its agony. Job knew what it was and he knew that it was not something foreign to humanity, for he said, "His flesh upon him shall have pain."

There is another kind of suffering Job knew. He not only said, "His flesh upon him shall have pain," but he added, "and his soul within him shall mourn." In Job's case and in many others this is the type of pain and suffering that is most dreaded. Isaiah spoke of having pain from just seeing and hearing (21:3). Such suffering can be terribly real. It makes one toss and turn in the night. Bad news about our children can do this to us. Seeing those we love do things that lead to tragedy will also do this to us, especially if we cannot say a word to them about it.

Jeremiah knew what it was to have heart pain (4:19). It came to him because he heard the sound of the trumpets and the alarm of war. This is the kind of suffering that many have known through the years and generations. David spoke of his heart being sore pained within him (Ps. 55:4).

Why should there be such suffering and pain? Why the agony of heart? Why the groaning of the soul? Why the recurring aches and pains of life which grind away at our bodies and spirits?

I often do not know the answer when people ask me these questions. I have seen much suffering for which I knew no answer whatsoever. I have had to face persons with broken hearts and say, "I do not know why this thing happened." It is not only difficult but sometimes utterly impossible for us to read the meaning of our tears.

One thing that ought to be settled here is that pain and suffering are not necessarily the result of some personal sin on the part of the sufferer. There is a general line of teaching abroad that suffering is invariably connected with some sin or wrong doing on the part of the sufferer. No wonder that when such afflicted persons honestly search in their lives for a reason for their condition and can find none they are frustrated. Moreover we must remember that those of us who have trusted in Christ have been forgiven all our sins. God does not reach into the past in an arbitrary manner to punish us for sins that are under the blood of Christ.

When we think suffering is the result of some specific sin, and we find no sin on which we can place our finger, there follows a feeling that God has turned against us and does not hear our pleas. We get the feeling that we are forsaken and alone in our trouble. There is more to it than this, however. Suffering is never in proportion to sin. Even the best of men know pain and grief. The Lord Jesus set this matter straight for us when the disciples asked Him concerning a blind man. "Who did sin, this man, or his parents, that he was born blind?" (John 9:2). It must have been a very surprised group who heard Jesus say, "Neither." Then He proceeded to explain the reason the man was born blind was that "the works of God should be made manifest in him" (John 9:3).

It is well to remember that pain does not always lead men to righteousness. We have all known persons who, the more they suffered, the more wicked they seemed to become. A classic example of this is found in Revelation 16:10: "And the fifth angel poured out his vial upon the seat of the beast; and his kingdom was full of darkness; and they gnawed their tongues for pain."

Sometimes our pain and suffering is a result of our own neglect and ignorance and not direct punishment for some sin at all. If we overeat, or do not eat enough, we are bound to suffer. In some respects pain is a relative matter. Tests by medical men show that we all suffer about the same, only some people react differently. A fighter in the ring will take quite a beating and come out smiling; but if his wife should accidentally bump him he may carry on as though he had been badly hurt.

The conclusion of the matter is, that if pain and suffering are present with us from no cause of our own, and there is no cure from man or God for it, then we must lift our eyes above the hills in absolute confidence and trust in God. When the enemy comes in like a flood, then it is that the Lord will lift up a standard against him. It is in the darkness that we may reach out our hand to God and know that He is by our side. The assurance that He holds us in His hand is better than a light shed on our pathway. We are safer in that case than if we walked on a well-worn path. It is then that we can say with confidence: "Be still; He who holds the worlds is holding thee!" We may not know what God intends, but we know that He knows and that His way is best for us! In order to get a proper perspective on pain and suffering, we must take a look not only at what is past but on into eternity:

> Life is real, life is earnest,
> And the grave is not the goal;
> Dust thou art, to dust returnest,
> Was not spoken of the soul.

While it is not easy for anyone who is passing through suffering to see this truth, we must remember that our future does not depend upon what we see or what we feel, but upon what God says. The Captain of our Salvation, the Lord Jesus Christ, suffered, and He sympathizes keenly with us in our suffering. Christ suffered in order that repentance and remissions of sins should be preached in His name among all nations (Luke 24:47). He suffered also in order that He might know our suffering and be a faithful high priest in representing us before the Father (Heb. 2:10-18).

The future is as bright as the promises of God, and one of these promises is, "If we suffer, we shall also reign with him: if we deny him, he also will deny us" (II Tim. 2:12). And "if children (of God) then heirs; heirs of God, and joint-heirs with Christ; if so be that we suffer with him, that we may be also glorified together. For I reckon that the sufferings of this present time are not worthy to be compared with the glory which shall be revealed in us" (Rom. 8:17,18).

Let us also remember that the day is coming when pain will be no more: "And God shall wipe away all tears from their eyes; and there shall be no more death, neither sorrow, nor crying, neither shall there be any more pain: for the former things are passed away" (Rev. 21:4).

> Light after darkness, gain after loss,
> Strength after weakness, crown after cross;
> Sweet after bitter, hope after fears,
> Home after wondering, praise after tears.

Sheaves after sowing, sun after rain,
Sight after mystery, peace after pain;
Joy after sorrow, calm after blast,
Rest after weariness, sweet rest at last.

Near after distant, gleam after gloom,
Love after loneliness, life after tomb;
After long agony, rapture of bliss—
Right was the pathway leading to this.

—Frances Havergal

Chapter Two

WHAT IS MAN?

Another great question raised by the Patriarch Job was this: "What is man?" Though Job was at times in despair (and who can blame him?); nevertheless, he caught glimpses of truths too wonderful for him to fully grasp. When he asked, "What is man?" it was not so much man himself that was in his view as why it was God paid so much attention to man. "What is man, that thou shouldest magnify him? and that thou shouldest set thine heart upon him? And that thou shouldest visit him every morning, and try him every moment? How long wilt thou not depart from me, nor let me alone till I swallow down my spittle (for a breathing spell)? I have sinned; what shall I do unto thee, O thou preserver of men? why hast thou set me as a mark against thee, so that I am a burden to myself?" (Job 7:17-20).

Job saw what we need to see, that man is a special creation of God. He magnifies man sometimes, sets His heart upon him, tests him, visits him, and preserves him. To say, as does the evolutionist, that man is a thinking animal, a creature left to the mercy of his needs, urges and drives, is never a satisfactory answer to the puzzle, "What is man?"

To say that man is a product of chance, change and environment and that through some miracle of evolution man became man, is equally unsatisfactory. A man may be deceived into accepting that idea when he is swollen with pride and wants all creation to think he is responsible to no one. But when he is all alone, when night has wrapped him in darkness, when his mind wanders out beyond the stars, he craves a better answer than that his ancestors were anteaters! His soul, though sold to the powers of darkness, is yet able to knock on the gates of heaven and to long for the light that he knows he was created to share in. You get this man in a corner, put pressure on him, drive him until he reaches his wit's end, and he will look for help, not to an animal ancestry, but to God! You see,

> Man is more than iron dug from central gloom,
> And heated hot with burning fears,
> And dipt in baths of hissing tears,
> And battered with the shocks of doom.

Man is a creature that can leap into the arms of God, for he bears God's image. We were made to love God, and we are never quite all we should be until we do love Him.

We are conscious of the fact, as was the Psalmist, that we are fearfully and wonderfully made; that we are more than bone, muscle, skin, hair and blood. To observe our bodies at work, one might be tempted to say that man consists of a ceaseless motion of chemical substances — and that is all some persons see. But deep down in our

18

hearts none of us are persuaded that this is the total man!

We call man a number of things. We say he is the animal that laughs, and that he laughs and builds houses and worries. Or, as some have said, "Man is that being who is always in a hurry so that he may have some time saved up to waste!" But man is more than meets the eye. When we look at a man, we do not see all that there is to him. To say that man is just what we see, is to face the frustration of the old philosopher who dreamed that he was a beautiful butterfly. Then he worried because he was not sure if he was a man dreaming that he was a butterfly, or if he really was a butterfly dreaming that he was a man!

The problem is not, as we noted at the beginning, "What is man?" That is not as hard to answer as we sometimes think it is. The thing that stimulated Job's wonder was, "What is man that God would magnify him?" Why should God bother about a man in any case? Why did God consider Job and test him and preserve him? Why did God not merely let him die?

The answer to this was beginning to break like an eternal light on the mind of Job. Man was more than so many pounds of flesh! Job realized that man was more than a changeful and fitful flame, kindled and then put out like a light in the night. Man had a relationship to God. God had set His heart upon him. So Job's question was, "Why should this be so?"

To be loved is the greatest thing that can happen to a man on earth. It has been said, and I believe it, that a man cannot live without love. Then to think that God loves us and has set His heart upon us, that is cause for wonder indeed! This was an exciting revelation to Job. It is to anyone and everyone who can and will grasp it.

David looked into the heavens, and the wonders of man's relationship with God set him so aflame that he sang: "When I consider thy heavens, the work of thy fingers, the moon and the stars, which thou hast ordained; What is man, that thou art mindful of him? and the son of man, that thou visitest him? For thou hast made him a little lower than the angels, and hast crowned him with glory and honour. Thou madest him to have dominion over the works of thy hands; thou hast put all things under his feet: All sheep and oxen, yea, and the beasts of the field; The fowl of the air, and the fish of the sea, and whatsoever passeth through the paths of the seas. O Lord our Lord, how excellent is thy name in all the earth!" (Ps. 8:3-9).

Man is a creature of life, but it is life such as no other on earth. It is not something that can be seen in a microscope. The surgeon's knife can never dissect it, and no biologist can ever find it. It is God-breathed life, for it was into the body of Adam that God breathed, and man became a living soul.

Man, then, is God's special creation. God set His heart upon him. This should be welcome relief to those who have been in trouble and despair, who have known weakness and frustration. All is not lost. Matters are not out of the hands of God. There is no need to give way to fear, nor let the darkness swallow us up. God has set His heart upon us!

The puzzle, "What is Man?" is really no puzzle at all

—or if it is, it is a puzzle of our own making. It can be solved the very instant that we acknowledge that man is the direct creation of God.

There is a stamp upon man that no other earthly creature bears. Man can be many things. He can be mighty, mischievous, cruel, foolish, angry, strong, weak, brutish, wicked, happy, sad, evil, violent, vain, wise, prudent, slothful, thrifty, diligent, angry or docile. He can be more. He can pray with some inexplainable sense of an unseen presence, and he can praise, sing, worship and believe! God made him so.

God magnified man and set His heart upon him. That is why man should not live by bread alone, which would be enough were man composed only of a body. But he is to live by every word that proceedeth out of the mouth of God. Unless man does so, he will not live as he should. He will be living below the will of God and will miss out on the blessings God intended for him.

What then is man? He is the special creation, the king of all God's creatures! Man is a creature of God's love. Man's creation was not the result of a hasty decision by God. Man was the product of the will and the love of God. God made him to love Him and made him so that man could love God. This is expressed in the Song of Solomon in these words: "He brought me to the banqueting house, and his banner over me was love" (2:4). Part of the wonder of God's love is revealed in the fact that He loved us before He created us. In his letter of encouragement to the Ephesian church Paul said, "Blessed be the God and Father of our Lord Jesus Christ, who hath blessed us with all spiritual blessings in heavenly places in Christ: According as he hath chosen us in him before the foundation of the world, that we should be holy and without blame before him in love" (1:3,4).

God has not turned His heart away from us now. He still loves us. "In this was manifested the love of God toward us, because that God sent his only begotten Son into the world, that we might live through him. Herein is love, not that we loved God, but that he loved us, and sent his Son to be the propitiation (atoning sacrifice) for our sins. Beloved, if God so loved us, we ought also to love one another" (I John 4:9-11).

In addition to this we have assurance from the Lord through Paul that He will always love us: "Whom he called, them he also justified: and whom he justified, them he also glorified. What shall we then say to these things? If God be for us, who can be against us? He that spared not his own Son; but delivered him up for us all, how shall he not with him also freely give us all things? Who shall lay anything to the charge of God's elect? It is God that justifieth. Who is he that condemneth? It is Christ that died, yea rather, that is risen again, who is even at the right hand of God, who also maketh intercession for us. Who shall separate us from the love of Christ? shall tribulation, or distress, or persecution, or famine, or nakedness, or peril, or sword? As it is written, For thy sake we are killed all the day long; we are accounted as sheep for the slaughter. Nay, in all these things we are more than conquerors through him that loved us. For I am persuaded, that neither death, nor life, nor angels, nor principalities, nor powers, nor things present, nor things to come, Nor height, nor depth, nor any other creature, shall be able to separate us from the love of God, which is in Christ Jesus our Lord" (Rom. 8:30-39).

God loved man and showed it by watching over him. This is sufficiently illustrated for us by the fact that Noah and his family were saved from the judgment of the flood and were preserved to replenish the earth following the flood. Abraham was called from the darkness and idolatry of a heathen land and placed in the land of promise. When the enemies of God sought to destroy Daniel in the lion's den, God intervened. And what clearer illustration of the love of God is there than Israel scattered among the nations and yet preserved and once again taking a part among the family of nations.

Not only did God love man and watch over him, but He provided the price of redemption for him when he sinned. All the sacrifices and types of the Old Testament were pictures teaching that Christ would come and be the world's Redeemer. It was in Christ that the full price of man's redemption was met: "In whom we have redemption through his blood, the forgiveness of sins, according to the riches of his grace" (Eph. 1:7). "But Christ being come an high priest of good things to come . . . by his own blood he entered in once into the holy place, having obtained eternal redemption for us" (Heb. 9:11,12).

This confronts us with a new slant to the puzzle of Job when he asked, "What is man?" The question to be answered now is, "Why does man go his own way when God has provided all he needs for salvation, peace, joy, and a future of bliss? Pope, in his essay on man, said it well:

Oh sons of earth! Attempt ye still to rise,
  By mountains piled on mountains, to the skies?
Heaven still with laughter the vain toil surveys,
  And buries madmen in the heaps they raise.

The way to God is found, fashioned and fixed. There
is no other! God made us, loved us, redeemed us through
His Son, and now gives the invitation to all: "Whosoever
will, let him come unto me and live."

We cannot put one little star in motion,
  We cannot shape one single forest leaf,
We cannot fling a mountain up, nor sink an ocean.
  Presumptuous pigmy, large with unbelief!

We cannot bring one dawn of regal splendor,
  Nor bid the day to shadowy twilight fall,
Nor send the pale moon forth with radiance tender;
  And dare we doubt the One who has done all?

—*S. A. Nagel*

"He that cometh to God must believe that he is, and
that he is a rewarder of them that diligently seek him"
(Heb. 11:6).

Chapter Three

HOW SHALL A MAN BE JUST WITH GOD?

Job's friend, Bildad, argued that Job's afflictions were due to his sins. Bildad voiced his opinion in this fashion: "Doth God pervert judgment? or doth the Almighty pervert justice? (Bildad knew as did Job that God always gives right judgment and justice.) If thy children have sinned against him, and he hath cast them away for their transgression; If thou wouldest seek unto God betimes, and make thy supplication to the Almighty; If thou wert pure and upright; surely now he would awake for thee, and make the habitation of thy righteousness prosperous . . . Behold, God will not cast away a perfect man, neither will he help the evildoers: Till he fill thy mouth with laughing, and thy lips with rejoicing. They that hate thee shall be clothed with shame; and the dwelling place of the wicked shall come to nought" (Job 8:3-6, 20-22).

In seeking an answer to Bildad's accusation of hypocrisy, Job must have thought back to the days of his worship, as recorded in chapter 1. If the sacrifices that Job offered did not avail, then he might well ask, "How shall a man be just with God?"

Job then looked at the relationship between himself and God and faced his own situation honestly and tried to evaluate things properly. According to the third verse of the 9th chapter he realized that a man cannot argue with God—not one in a thousand could answer Him! Then according to verse 4 Job saw that if men hardened their hearts against God, they were the losers, for the the strength of God is far beyond man's comprehension. God can remove mountains. He can shake the earth and make its very foundations tremble (vv. 5,6). God is near but man does not see Him (v. 11). He takes away from man and no one can hinder Him. He did this with Job and, as absolute King, He had the right to do so! (v. 12).

Job does not confine himself to this line of thought. He knows that he cannot argue with God and that he is not righteous enough to question the acts of the Lord. Job fell back on the mercy of God when he said, "I would make supplication to my judge" (v. 15). Look well to this statement, for it contains the key to how any man can have a right relationship with God.

Continuing to think on his problem, Job said, "If I speak of strength, lo, he is strong: and if of judgment, who shall set me a time to plead? If I justify myself, mine own mouth shall condemn me: if I say, I am perfect, it shall also prove me perverse" (9:19,20). He saw that the days of his life were flying by, "Swifter than a post" and as the "swift ships," and as the "eagle that hasteth to the prey." He can neither forget nor ignore his past, for well he knows that God cannot overlook it. He continues his thinking out loud by saying, "If I wash myself with snow water, and make my hands never so clean; Yet shalt thou plunge me in the ditch, and mine own clothes shall abhor me. For he is not a man, as I am, that I should answer him, and we should come together in judgment" (vv. 30,31).

It is then that the solution to this puzzle is given to Job. He sees there must be someone who can mediate between God and man: "Neither is there any daysman betwixt us, that might lay his hand upon us both. Let him take his rod away from me, and let not his fear terrify me: Then would I speak, and not fear him; but it is not so with me" (vv. 33-35). This, then, is the answer to the question, "How can a man be just with God?" Someone must be found who can "Lay his hand upon us both." It must be someone who is at home in the presence of God and at the same time is at home among men. It must be someone who is as righteous as God, and yet someone who can stand in the presence of God as a man. If such a person could be found, then men could speak with God and not fear!

Job was not the first nor the last to think on the question of how man can be just with God. This is a matter that must have occupied the minds of all men at one time or another. It may not have been expressed in these words, but it was thought of just the same.

It is not popular to think such thoughts out loud today. This is a day of self-worship, so men do not speak as openly on this subject as they may have in other ages, but they think on it nevertheless.

See the dilemma we have created for ourselves trying to act as if there was no problem of sin at all! First of all, we try to convince ourselves that there is no God. We say that the world got here by chance and that man got here by being at the right place at the right time, and

27

he, too, is the product of chance and environment. Somehow by the exercise of our own will, we changed from one thing to another, from ants to alligators and from apes to Adam! By this line of reasoning we leave God out. He is not needed as Creator. Logically then, and of course we want to be logical in all things, there is no sin, no heaven, no hell, no judgment. As the dog dies, so does a man die and all this matter of justice and concern with what God thinks, turns out to be merely old wives' tales. So there is not much to life and there is nothing to death. All that is left is for us to eat and drink and be merry, for tomorrow we die. That is all there is to life—so we would like to think.

Still, we are not convinced by our own arguments. Whistling in the dark does not remove reality from us. We have a conscience and we cannot get rid of it. It is a moral sense, a feeling of right and wrong, something we cannot shake. We look for an answer concerning its source. We find that a conscience can be seared, or wounded until it does not respond as it should, but there is always something of it left.

Then there is God's miracle people, the people of the ages, known to us as Israel. Their presence must be accounted for. They cannot be explained away. In fact, they cannot be explained at all without recognizing the hand of God in history.

There is also God's miracle book, the Bible. In this great volume the prophets spoke of unborn history with the same assurance as if they were sitting at the unfolding scene with pen in hand, writing the events transpiring before them. When they wrote of coming events, they were not right only part of the time, but all of the time.

Then we always come back to the subject of our origin. We are not quite able to make ourselves believe that we came from nowhere, that we are nothing now, and that we are going nowhere to lose forever whatever identity we might have as individuals. There is a tiny suspicion of doubt in all of our hearts on this subject. For most persons it is more than a doubt, it is conviction based upon reason, history and revelation that we are creatures of the Great Creator. He is the Lord of heaven and earth, the One who made the worlds and who upholds all things by the Word of His power. He formed man and breathed into his nostrils the breath of life, and man became a living soul.

We are not creatures of chance who came into the world for a moment to live, laugh, weep, suffer, beget children and then die, knowing only the divinity of dust! We are here as the creation of God, and His desire is to make us His children by faith. We were created for His glory and for His fellowship and for His love!

> "I lean upon the garden wall,
>   And looking on my garden small,
>   These foolish words I then recall:
>   Some men contend that God is naught!
>   Not God? In gardens? When the eve is cool?
>   No God to fashion rose and vine?
>   Ah, this I know, from time to time,
>   God walks in mine!"

Another of our difficulties is that if we cannot persuade ourselves that there is no God, then we try to mold Him into a God that suits our own way of thinking. We want a God whom we can manipulate, One who lets us do as we please, One who never crosses us or hinders us in our selfish ways, nor will He judge us in the end. We like to remind ourselves that God is good, so good, in fact, that He will not call our lives into question or bring us into judgment for our sin. It follows then that if He is so good, He will not rebuke us for our rebellion or discipline us for our disobedience. We do not object to calling Him "Lord, Lord," as long as we do not really make Him Lord.

If this does not work, then we seek to define sin to suit our taste. "Sin is not really sin," we say with our tongue in our cheek, "It is just an unfortunate mistake." We are not really bad, that is, we are not sinners by nature, for what we do that is wrong is merely an error of judgment and nothing more. We can remind God that we meant no harm, and if He is the kind of God we have conjured in our minds, He will dismiss the whole matter with a smile. He may even give us a sympathetic pat on the head and tell us to forget the whole affair.

But this is not the way things are—and we know it! Our deeds, past and present, betray us. We have warred in our hearts toward our neighbors and toward God. The present world situation is a graphic testimony to all of that. We are jealous, our hearts are full of hate, and this leads to murder. We are full of guile, we are lustful, idolatrous, unfaithful, proud, discontented with God's ways, covetous, foolish, unthankful, deceitful, unrighteous, wicked, malicious, envious, backbiters, despiteful, boasters and inventors of evil. By nature we have no natural affection and are blasphemers, disobedient, truce breakers, despisers of those that are good!

No! It will not do for us to stand before our record and apologetically say, "I am sorry, I merely made a little mistake, I did not mean it at all." Our excuses will not do. God will not accept them. He demands justice, and we know we stand condemned as Job well knew. There is none righteous, no not one. We are guilty. Our mouths are stopped. We must find someone who can lay his hand upon us and upon God and find a ground of reconciliation, or we perish. Job knew this (9:33), and so do we!

Many thinking men, many well-known men and great men, as we count greatness, have admitted that their accountability to God had demanded their serious attention. Faced with the right circumstances, each of us, whether we will admit it or not, has wrestled with this question: "How can a man be just with God?"

In this question raised by Job there is, first of all, a confession of need. The confession may not be universal, but the need certainly is. This is also the first step toward a solution of our estrangement from God. Jesus said, "I am come to seek and to save that which was lost." The lost He speaks of here are the lost who would admit it and seek help. People in His own day He warned: "You would not come to me that you might have life." These would not admit their need. Yet death was everywhere; the wages of sin were in evidence all about them, but these persons would not admit it. This is why our Lord said in another place: "I have not come to call the righteous, but sinners to repentance."

This is a day of great tensions. There is frustration

no matter where we look. This is a time of great sorrow. There are many people who know that life is short and that sin is in their hearts and all about them. They are weary and tired of this load. They have wept and prayed, but up till now have found no peace. If you are such, take heart, for the admission of your need is the first step to your help.

Job's question is also an admission of a lack. Something has gone wrong in the human race. Something has made it necessary that we re-establish right relationships with God. This is a confession of a lack of power in man to right what is wrong. Jeremiah spoke of this when he said, "It is not within man to direct his own steps." Isaiah pointed out this same truth when he said, "All we like sheep have gone astray." Job was fully aware of this when he stated that there needed to be a "daysman," a "go-between," a "negotiator," "a mediator," someone to plead his cause for him.

Job was no stranger to what had happened in human hearts. He knew the history of rebellion in the human race. This was the reason he was so careful to offer the prescribed sacrifices that God demanded in his day. He knew that there was a time when man had stood face to face with God. He knew that at one time God and man had walked and talked together. Once there was sweet fellowship between the Creator and the creature. Once there was a time when man enjoyed listening to the voice of God, gloried in His presence and basked in His smile. But Job also knew that rebellion had sprung up in the heart of man and through rebellion, fellowship with God had been broken. Sin had entered, and death by sin.

Death was something Job saw before his very eyes. His sheep and their attendants had been burned up. His camels were taken away and his servants slain. His sons and his daughters were dead. He knew from the past history of the flood that the wages of sin is death; but he also knew from the events of the present that the wages of sin were still being gathered. Now he went to the heart of the matter and wanted to know how man can stand before God again and know His forgiveness and enjoy His fellowship. He asked, "How shall a man be just with God?"

The gospel is the answer to Job's question. Paul says it in this fashion: "Wherefore, as by one man sin entered into the world, and death by sin; and so death passed upon all men, for that all have sinned . . . Therefore as by the offence of one judgment came upon all men to condemnation; even so by the righteousness of one the free gift came upon all men unto justification of life. For as by one man's disobedience many were made sinners, so by the obedience of one shall many be made righteous. Moreover the law entered, that the offence might abound. But where sin abounded, grace did much more abound: That as sin hath reigned unto death, even so might grace reign through righteousness unto eternal life by Jesus Christ our Lord" (Rom. 5:12, 18-21).

The "daysman" that Job sought is Jesus Christ, the Mediator between man and God. As man He shared our sorrows and became acquainted with our grief; as God He paid redemption's price for us. He alone can lay His hand upon us as we receive Him and His righteousness and present us faultless before God (Jude 24).

Have you been justified before God by putting your
faith, your confidence, your trust in Jesus Christ?

Chapter Four

WHAT IS JUSTIFICATION?

It is little short of amazing the progress that man has made in these last years. For example, for thousands of years the fastest any person could travel was the speed of a good horse. Now we can fly from one place to another at speeds of 500 miles an hour and more. In nearly any field of endeavor we can point with pride to our achievements. Nevertheless, if we are willing to face things as they really are, there are two areas in which we have made no advance whatsoever. These are our relationships with each other and our relationship with God. Men still fight with men and men still rebel against God. Our problem is a heart problem and all our scientific progress has not changed that.

One reason we are not able to cope with this problem is that we start at the wrong end. We try to get right with our neighbor before we are right with God. Many of us are guilty of teaching our children how to be good neighbors without ever teaching them how they can be right with God and have their hearts changed so that we can make good progress in both realms. We soon discover for ourselves and our children that as long as our hearts are filled with pride and selfish desires and self-will that we do not even get along with our families.

The Lord Jesus Christ put these matters in their proper order when in condensing the Law into two main categories He said, "Thou shalt love the Lord thy God with all thy heart, and with all thy soul, and with all thy mind . . . and . . . thou shalt love thy neighbour as thyself" (Matt. 22:37,39). To have right relationship with God is first. This is essential for all of life, be it social, economic, political or spiritual. When a man's physical heart is bad there are some things that he cannot do, for his heart will not stand the strain. When his spiritual heart, that is, the very center of his being, is bad, it is impossible for him to do the right thing. His heart will not let him. It is imperative then, that our hearts be made right with God first.

When Job asked the question, "How shall a man be just with God?" he asked that which is fundamental to living right in this world. If we can find how we can be just with God, there is hope for us. If not, we will be left to muddle along as we have been in our mixed-up condition of madness and misery.

Let us first discover what it is we are seeking when we want to be just with God. What is justification? What do we mean when we speak of being just with God? To be justified means to be declared righteous; to be declared upright; to be declared legally right. So then, to be just with God means that even though we have sinned and are guilty, yet a verdict is rendered in our favor, declaring us righteous before God. Job's question is this: "How can this be?" Before we can be just in God's sight some way must be found whereby God can pardon our past because we are guilty, forgive our sins because we are sinners, and still be just.

A judge may feel sorry for a criminal standing before him in court and may want to pardon him, but the judge must find some grounds upon which the lawbreaker can be legally pardoned. If not, then the judge must sentence him to pay the penalty demanded by the law. In the case of God's law the penalty of sin is death. This is what God has stipulated and this law cannot be broken if God is to remain just. God must remain faithful to that law, for He has established Himself as being just. Isaiah made this plain when he said to the Lord's people Israel: "Assemble yourselves and come; draw near together, ye that are escaped of the nations: they have no knowledge that set up the wood of their graven image, and pray unto a god that cannot save. Tell ye, and bring them near; yea, let them take counsel together: who hath declared this from ancient time? who hath told it from that time? have not I the Lord? and there is no God else beside me; a just God and a Saviour; there is none beside me" (45: 20,21).

Daniel prayed, "O Lord, righteousness belongeth unto thee" (Dan. 9:7). Since God is just, He must either find a way to pardon man and to declare him righteous, or He must carry out on the man the sentence of death for sin. Moses said of God, "He is the Rock, his work is perfect: for all his ways are judgment: a God of truth and without iniquity, just and right is he" (Deut. 32:4).

The factor we so often overlook is that the sentence of death is already passed upon all men because all have sinned. This penalty could be carried out on every person and God would be perfectly just in exacting it. Not one particle of censure could be brought against Him. So then, it is not justice we must plead, but mercy. It is mercy, and mercy alone, that caused God to seek and to find a way that would make it possible for man to stand before God in righteousness and peace.

How could this be done? How did God provide for us in order that we may be just before Him? How can God let the guilty go free and still remain just? Or to put it another way, How can God declare sinners righteous? The answer lies in what we call the gospel—the good news, for good news indeed it is!

The plan God has used through the ages and uses today, is simplicity itself. Do not think that because it is simple, it is worthless. Some of us are inclined to think that unless something is complex and difficult it is not good. This plan is all God requires and is, therefore, all that you and I should ask for, even though it is simple.

God came into the world in the person of His Son, Jesus Christ, to be man's Redeemer. The four Gospels, the first four books of the New Testament, tell the story of His coming. They record the account of His life and of His death and of His resurrection. In Him was no sin. This was testified of by the Father and by Christ's disciples. Since He was sinless, there never was a sentence of death upon Him. The sentence of death came upon mankind because of sin, but the Son, being perfect, offered Himself as the divine substitute to die in the place of guilty man. Therefore, in His death, the law is satisfied, since it demanded the death of man. And the

38

man who was sentenced to death; that is, you and I, can go free. The penalty assessed against us has been fully paid.

There are conditions to be met for each person who will be justified before God. This is not a gift given to the human race automatically even though God has provided it for all. The condition God demands is our confession that we have sinned. This is an admission of our guilt. This is to be followed with repentance, which is a turning away from sin to God and includes a willingness to make Christ Lord of all. This is what makes Him your Saviour or my Saviour. This is what is meant by "believing" on the Lord. To believe means a personal turning from our sin and a personal acknowledging of Christ as Lord because of His death for us on the cross. He now lives to be our Lord. This is why Paul said, "God forbid that I should glory, save in the cross of our Lord Jesus Christ." It is not enough that we recognize Him as being "a" Saviour. We must come to the place where we can say of Him, "He is MY Saviour."

This is not all that takes place in this process. The righteousness of Christ is set to the account of the one who believes and receives Christ as Lord. Our record says, "Guilty and deserving of death." His record says, "Not guilty," and therefore, He sets all of His righteousness to our account. This is vividly illustrated in the life of Abraham, according to Romans 4. Here is what Paul wrote: "What shall we say then that Abraham our father, as pertaining to the flesh, hath found? For if Abraham were justified by works, he hath whereof to glory; but not before God. For what saith the scripture?

Abraham believed God, and it was counted unto him for righteousness" (Rom. 4:1-3).

The apostle goes on to tell us that Abraham "staggered not at the promises of God through unbelief; but was strong in faith, giving glory to God; and being fully persuaded that, what he had promised, he was able also to perform. And therefore it was imputed to him for righteousness. Now it was not written for his sake alone, that it was imputed to him; But for us also, to whom it shall be imputed, if we believe on him that raised up Jesus our Lord from the dead; Who was delivered for our offences, and was raised again for our justification" (Rom. 4:20-25).

God raised Christ from the dead as proof to all thinking creatures in the universe that Christ's sacrifice was accepted before God. Because of this the Scriptures declare: "What shall we then say to these things? If God be for us, who can be against us? He that spared not his own Son, but delivered him up for us all, how shall he not with him also freely give us all things? Who shall lay anything to the charge of God's elect? It is God that justifieth. Who is he that condemneth? It is Christ that died, yea rather, that is risen again, who is even at the right hand of God, who also maketh intercession for us" (Rom. 8:31-34).

This is not the end of these matters. The grace of God is "abundant grace." God did more than justify us on the grounds of Christ's death for us. He did more than set to our account the righteousness of Christ on our confession of faith in that work for us. He also sent the Holy Spirit to dwell in the heart of every believer, that we may have help, comfort and strength to act as God wants us to act.

Regeneration

We have seen that in justification the guilty sinner, through trusting in Christ, is declared righteous before God. Though this gives the believer a position before God, justification does not make the believer's conduct righteous in his everyday life among men. Another work of the Spirit of God does that. We call it regeneration. The Spirit of God creates in the human heart a divine nature. This produces in the believer the desire to do the things of God as Peter says in his second letter: "According as his divine power hath given unto us all things that pertain unto life and godliness, through the knowledge of him that hath called us to glory and virtue: Whereby are given unto us exceeding great and precious promises: that by these ye might be partakers of the divine nature, having escaped the corruption that is in the world through lust" (II Pet. 1:3,4).

In order to give us power to do that which the new nature within us desires, God has given us the Holy Spirit to indwell us. Concerning this Paul wrote to the Corinthian believers: "What! know ye not that your body is the temple of the Holy Ghost which is in you, which ye have of God, and ye are not your own? For ye are bought with a price: therefore glorify God in your body, and in your spirit, which are God's" (I Cor. 6:19,20).

You may well ask, "But how can we glorify God in our bodies? The old habits still hold us. It is so easy for us to lose our tempers, for example. Remember, God's commands are His enablings; what He asks of us He provides power for us to do. The promise is, "For it is God which worketh in you both to will and to do of his good pleasure" (Phil. 2:13). This calls on us for full surrender to the Lord. When we accept all Christ is by faith, God can work out His purposes in us and through us.

Because of the strength of the Lord within us, Paul can admonish us to "Do all things without murmurings and disputings: That ye may be blameless and harmless, the sons of God, without rebuke, in the midst of a crooked and perverse nation, among whom ye shine as lights in the world; Holding forth the word of life; that I may rejoice in the day of Christ, that I have not run in vain, neither laboured in vain" (Phil. 2:14-16).

That which we call Christian graces are actually the fruit of the Spirit which are developed in us as the result of our surrender to Him. Galatians 5:22-26 bears this out: "But the fruit of the Spirit is love, joy, peace, longsuffering, gentleness, goodness, faith, Meekness, temperance: against such there is no law. And they that are Christ's have crucified the flesh with the affections and lusts. If we live in the Spirit, let us also walk in the Spirit. Let us not be desirous of vain glory, provoking one another, envying one another."

Both regeneration and justification are brought together in Paul's letter to Titus. The apostle wrote: "But after that the kindness and love of God our Saviour toward man appeared, Not by works of righteousness which we have done, but according to his mercy he saved us, by the washing of regeneration, and renewing of the Holy Spirit; Which he shed on us abundantly through Jesus Christ our Saviour; That being justified by his grace, we should be made heirs according to the hope of eternal life" (3:4-7).

So then, justification gives us a right standing before God. It places to our account the righteousness of Jesus Christ, the righteous One. Then, God gives us a divine nature through the work of the Holy Spirit. He also gives us the Holy Spirit to live in us so that we may do the things that please Him.

These, then, are some of the things that are involved in being a Christian.

My Hiding Place

Hail, sovereign love, which first began;
The scheme to rescue fallen man!
Hail, matchless, free, eternal grace,
Which gave my soul a hiding place.

Against the God that built the sky
I fought with hands uplifted high,
Despised the mention of His grace,
Too proud to seek a hiding place.

Enwrapt in thick Egyptian night,
And fond of darkness more than light,
Madly I ran the sinful race,
Secure—without a hiding place!

But thus the eternal counsel ran;
Almighty love, arrest that man!
I felt the arrows of distress,
And found I had no hiding place.

Indignant justice stood in view;
To Sinai's fiery mount I flew;
But justice cried with frowning face,
This mountain is no hiding place!

Ere long a heavenly voice I heard,
And mercy's angel soon appeared:
He led me with a beaming face,
To JESUS as a hiding place.

On Him almighty vengeance fell,
Which must have sunk a world to hell!
He bore it for a sinful race,
And thus became their Hiding Place.

Should sevenfold storms of thunder roll,
And shake this globe from pole to pole,
No thunderbolt shall daunt my face,
For JESUS is my Hiding Place.

—*Major John Andre*

Chapter Five

SOME IMMEDIATE RESULTS OF JUSTIFICATION

A great evangelist of the past generation by the name of Gypsy Smith, thinking of the mercy and grace of God in making justification possible, wrote, "If I am dreaming, let me dream on." But he was not dreaming and he knew it! Justification is a glad and glorious possibility for us all.

How pitiful it is in the light of God's provisions for men that some will say, when questioned concerning their eternal destiny, "Well, I am doing my best. I hope it is good enough; but if it isn't, I will just have to take that chance." What a dreadful way to live, never knowing, never sure, merely hoping that all will turn out right in the end. The fact is, if good works, right resolves and earnest efforts could have given us justification before God, Christ would not have had to die in order to provide it. The sentence of death is upon all of us, and our best is not enough to annul that sentence.

We live in an age that boasts of being practical. Heaven is something future, but like Peter, many of us want to know what there is for us in the Christian life here and now. When Peter raised this question, however, he had gone farther than many of us, for he said: "Behold, we have forsaken all, and followed thee; what shall we have therefore?" (Matt. 19:27). The Lord Jesus did not deal sharply with Peter for his question, but answered in these words: "Ye which have followed me, in the regeneration when the Son of man shall sit in the throne of his glory, ye also shall sit upon twelve thrones, judging the twelve tribes of Israel. And every one that hath forsaken houses, or brethren, or sisters, or father, or mother, or wife, or children, or lands, for my name's sake, shall receive an hundredfold, and shall inherit everlasting life" (Matt. 19:28,29).

The above has to do with some of the future results that flow from salvation, but what are some of the immediate results? In other words, does it pay to be a Christian now? Let me assure you that a life lived in right relationship with God through Jesus Christ is a life that grows better and brighter as we travel along life's path. The writer of Proverbs said, "The path of the just is as the shining light, that shineth more and more unto the perfect day" (Prov. 4:18). The way of the Lord does not lead to disappointment and despair. It is the way of deep joy and inner-satisfaction. Do not judge the Lord by some sour saint that you know. There can be a bad banana in any bunch. Judge the Lord by the promises and provisions He has made. Rest in His care, and live by faith. Lift up your eyes above the hills and you will find your help in God, and you will be able to go on your way rejoicing.

When we know we have been declared righteous with God, we have a new assurance in life. We need no longer go along in darkness fearful of what a day might bring forth. God does not forsake His own at any time. One of the most remarkable promises in the Bible is Hebrews 13:5. The Amplified Version brings out the force of the original: "For He (God) Himself has said, I will not in any way fail you nor give you up nor leave you without support. (I will) not (I will) not (I will) not, in any degree leave you helpless, nor forsake nor let (you) down, (relax my hold on you).—Assuredly not!" He is with us all through life to deliver us and keep us in His perfect will. Then, after this life is over, we have the assurance of His "welcome home."

When we have been declared righteous by God through faith in Jesus Christ, life is full of rich meaning. We can enjoy it knowing that it is not going to be filled with regrets. "The memory of the just is blessed" (Prov. 10:7). That is why Solomon wrote in Ecclesiastes 12:1: "Remember now thy Creator in the days of thy youth, while the evil days come not, nor the years draw nigh, when thou shalt say, I have no pleasure in them."

I remember working with a man one day during my first pastorate. We visited as we worked and after a while he became silent. I turned from what I was doing to speak to him and saw that he was crying. Thinking that he might possibly have injured himself severely by one of the tools that we were using I asked him if he had hurt himself.

"No," he replied, "I did not hurt myself, I have been thinking over my past life. You know, Pastor Morrow, I lived 50 years before I found Christ as my Saviour, and I was just crying over my wasted life."

I recall very vividly the first time I saw my father after he came to Christ. He was 70 years of age before he came to know the Lord Jesus Christ as his Saviour. We talked nearly the whole night through and the burden of his heart was, "Oh, son, why did I wait so long to be saved?"

I came to Christ at the age of 17. My only regret is that I did not come sooner. It is the life of justification with God that has no regrets and is filled with peace. This is what the Bible says: "Therefore being justified by faith, we have peace with God through our Lord Jesus Christ" (Rom. 5:1).

> Tonight I look upon the sky and think of Thee
> Oh God, Creator of those myriad stars and of
>   vast space between;
> And yet inside the hollow of the hand which
>   made all these
> My soul finds repose and rest and peace.
>
> I see Thy mercy, limitless as space,
> I see Thy love and feel Thy close embrace;
> And though Thy presence fills the universe,
> Yet as close as hands and heart Thou art to me.
>
> —*Olga J. Weiss*

The justified life is a life of joy here and now. Yet, there are many people who suppose that the only place of joy and happiness and good times is heaven, and they want to go there when they die. They think that God interferes too much with their personal lives and takes the joy out of living and spoils their fun. So they want to wait until the last moment to prepare to go to heaven. They do not want what they call "religion" to interfere with what they are doing now.

48

If by religion they mean that which has no life, no meaning and no joy, I could agree with them. There is nothing so boring as religion without Christ. But to have this attitude toward justification and Jesus Christ is to miss the point altogether. Jesus did not say that He had come to stifle our lives, or to bore us, or to make us miserable, or to take the zest from living. What He did say was, "I have come that ye might have life, and that ye might have it more abundantly." The more joy we have in life the more it pleases God.

At one time when the Lord was teaching His disciples, He said to them, "These things have I spoken unto you, that my joy might remain in you, and that your joy might be full" (John 15:11). He was telling them of His love for them and how they might have answered prayer and fruitful lives.

To have joy does not mean that we will feel like singing all the time—not unless we sing through tears. Life is not all song. It is mingled with toil, tears, testings and trials. However, we are reminded that no testing has come to us but such as is common to man, and God will not leave us without a way of escape (I Cor. 10:13).

Neither does joy mean that we will feel like breaking out into jubilant praise when we receive light on a subject we perhaps did not understand before. Our Lord was a man of joy, but He was not a man of frolic and light laughter, for these are not necessarily expressions of joy. Joy is a deep settled peace based upon the person and promises of God. Joy is knowing that all is well simply because God says so. The earth may be breaking up beneath us, but we trust in the everlasting arms under us. Joy is a foundation upon which we rest our hearts even when these hearts are broken. Joy is the assurance that God cares for us, that God loves us though men and the Devil may try to tell us it is not so. There will be times when they will say these very things to us. Joy is born out of the confidence we have in God who has promised that one day He will wipe away all tears from our eyes. Joyfully we wait and watch for that day even though we watch through tears, remembering that though weeping may endure for a night, joy comes in the morning (Ps. 30:5).

Joy is the settled fact that we are the children of God now, and that we have an inheritance with the saints of all ages. Joy is knowing that God commends His love toward us, in that, while we were yet sinners, Christ died for us. "Much more then, being now justified by his blood, we shall be saved from wrath through him. For if, when we were enemies, we were reconciled to God by the death of his Son, much more, being reconciled, we shall be saved by his life. And not only so, but we also joy in God through our Lord Jesus Christ, by whom we have now received the atonement" (Rom. 5:8-11).

> "O child of God, wait patiently,
>   When dark thy path may be,
> And let thy faith lean trustingly,
>   On Him who cares for Thee;
> And though the clouds hang drearily,
>   Upon the brow of night,
> Yet in the morning joy will come,
>   And fill the soul with light.

"O child of God, He loveth thee,
    And thou art all His own;
With gentle hand He leadeth thee,
    Thou dost not walk alone;
And though thou watchest wearily,
    The long and stormy night;
Yet in the morning joy will come,
    And fill thy soul with light.

"O child of God, how peacefully
    He calms thy fears to rest,
And draws thee upward tenderly,
    Where dwell the pure and blest;
And He who bendeth silently,
    Above the gloom of night,
Will take thee home where endless joy,
    Shall fill thy soul with light."

Another of the immediate results of justification is that we have a clean start and a clean life. In writing to the Corinthian Christians, Paul said, "Know ye not that the unrighteous shall not inherit the kingdom of God? Be not deceived: neither fornicators, nor idolaters, nor adulterers, nor effeminate, nor abusers of themselves with mankind, Nor thieves, nor covetous, nor drunkards, nor revilers, nor extortioners, shall inherit the kingdom of God. And such were some of you: but ye are washed, but ye are sanctified, but ye are justified in the name of the Lord Jesus, and by the Spirit of our God" (I Cor. 6:9-11).

I have heard people say that they would give anything

if only they could start life afresh. This, of course, none of us can do, for what is done is done, and we cannot undo it. God, however, in His infinite grace and unlimited mercy has so arranged it so that we can come to Him just as we are, and by repenting of our sins, be justified through faith in the shed blood of His Son. He will wash us and make us clean and give us a new start in life. Through Isaiah the Lord said centuries ago: "Come now, and let us reason together, saith the Lord: though your sins be of scarlet, they shall be as white as snow; though they be red like crimson, they shall be as wool" (1:18).

This life is filled with difficult problems. There are unseen pitfalls all along the way. There are subtle temptations that could bring our Christian testimony to ruin were we to give in to them. There is not one of us but who has tasted the bitterness of failure at one time or another. God, however, does not forsake His own. Another of the immediate results of justification is that we have an Advocate with the Father, a Go-between, One to plead our cause.

Our Advocate stands before God on our behalf. He lived here on earth for a while as we have lived, except for sin. He faced the same temptations we meet everyday. He lived among men and walked the common paths of life and met the tests that all men face. He was a man of sorrow and acquainted with grief. He knows the way we take and cares for us. The Spirit of God wrote about it in I John 2:1,2: "My little children, these things write I unto you, that ye sin not. And if any man sin, we have an advocate with the Father, Jesus Christ the righteous:

And he is the propitiation (atoning sacrifice) for our sins: and not for our's only, but also for the sins of the whole world."

> When this passing world is done,
> When has sunk yon glowing sun,
> When we stand with Christ in glory,
> Looking o'er life's finished story,
> Then, Lord, shall I fully know—
> Not till then—how much I owe.
>
> When I stand before the throne,
> Dressed in beauty not my own,
> When I see thee as Thou art,
> Love Thee with unsinning heart,
> Then, Lord, shall I fully know—
> Not till then—how much I owe.
>
> When the praise of heaven I hear,
> Loud as thunder to the ear,
> Loud as many water's noise,
> Sweet as harp's melodious voice,
> Then, Lord, shall I fully know—
> Not till then—how much I owe.
>
> Even on earth, as through a glass
> Darkly, let Thy glory pass,
> Make forgiveness feel so sweet,
> Make Thy Spirit's help to meet.
> Even on earth, Lord, make me know
> Something of how much I owe.

—*Robert Murray McCheyne*

Still another of the present and blessed benefits of being justified by faith with God is that now we may live in the will of God. It is only as we live in the will of God that we can be assured of enjoying the life of fullest joy. We are exhorted to live in God's will, according to Romans 12:2. "And be not conformed to this world," the apostle continues, "but be ye transformed by the renewing of your mind, that ye may prove what is that good, and acceptable, and perfect, will of God."

There are so many gracious by-products of living the justified life that one hardly knows where to start or stop. In Romans 12:3 we are admonished not to think more highly of ourselves than we ought to think. What a blessed relief this would be for thousands! Do we become disgusted and dissatisfied with our striving for status? Do we grow weary of trying to make people think we are something we actually are not? Sometimes our lives are consumed with trying to make people think that we are something better than we are.

Now to live the justified life does not mean we live foolishly, or slovenly. It does mean, however, that we can settle down to live simply, sensibly and soberly. It will not excite us whether people think one thing of us or another, for we will have the God-given ability to think of ourselves as we ought to think.

This in itself leads to a life that loves without any hypocrisy in it (Rom. 12:9). It is a life that can have kindly affection toward a brother in Christ no matter who he is or where he comes from, or what his station in life might be (Rom. 12:10). When the justified life is being expressed we are "not slothful in business; fervent in spirit; serving the Lord; Rejoicing in hope; patient in tribulation; continuing instant in prayer; Distributing to the necessity of saints; given to hospitality."

It is the justified life that allows us to bless "them which persecute us and to rejoice with those that do rejoice and to weep with those that weep."

The justified life means that we need not be wise in our own conceits, trying to impress others with our cleverness. It means that we do not seek to recompense to any man evil for evil. It means that we provide things honest in the sight of men. It means that we live peaceably as much as lieth in us with those around us. It means that we do not seek to avenge ourselves but rather give place unto wrath, because it is written, "Vengeance is mine; I will repay, saith the Lord" (Rom. 12:19). What a relief for a Christian to get rid of the "I will get even" spirit. I have known of family feuds that lasted so long that those who are carrying on the fight did not know what the original problem was all about.

The justified life also gives us something to work for. We seem to be natural builders, loving to show one another the things we have made. My father was a carpenter, and when I would visit him, he enjoyed taking me in an automobile through the town showing me the houses and buildings he had constructed. But we are building more than houses in this life. Paul tells us: "For other foundation can no man lay than that is laid, which is Jesus Christ. Now if any man build upon this foundation gold, silver, precious stones, wood, hay, stubble; Every man's work shall be made manifest: for the day shall declare it, because it shall be revealed by fire; and the fire shall try every man's work of what sort it is. If any man's work abide which he hath built thereupon, he shall receive a reward. If any man's work shall be burned, he shall suffer loss: but he himself shall be saved; yet so as by fire" (I Cor. 3:11-15).

Justification through faith in Christ who shed His blood for us gives us a solid foundation on which to build the best life possible. The building materials are gold, silver, and precious stones which, in the symbolism of the passage before us, would indicate a life lived in obedience to the will of God and in the power of God.

Part of the responsibility laid upon all believers by the Lord Jesus Christ is found in Matthew 28:19: "Go ye therefore, and teach all nations, baptizing them in the name of the Father, and of the Son, and of the Holy Ghost: Teaching them to observe all things whatsoever I have commanded you: and, lo, I am with you alway, even unto the end of the world (age)."

It is by our obedient walk with God that we build with these precious things, and it is also in this way that we preserve the service of our Christian lives for all eternity. One day our Lord said to the disciples: "If any man will come after me, let him deny himself, and take up his cross daily, and follow me. For whosoever will save his life shall lose it: but whosoever will lose his life for my sake, the same shall save it" (Luke 9:23,24). Surely it would be a terrible experience to come to the end of life and on looking back over it have to say, "All is wasted!" On the other hand, it will be an experience of deep joy to come to the end of life and in the presence of God say to

Him, "Father, we have lived this life for your sake and for your glory."

This kind of life is not confined only to those whom we often describe as being in full-time Christian service. This possibility and this responsibility is held out to all of God's people. Whether a man is a banker, lawyer, farmer, mechanic, doctor, preacher—if God is put first, then that life is saved in the sense spoken of by our Lord in Luke 9.

We are not creatures of the day. We are made for eternity. Out in those endless ages we will be individual personalities forever. The benefits of justification are not for the present only but for the eternal future. The Apostle John looking out into the future said, "Beloved, now are we the sons of God, and it doth not yet appear what we shall be: but we know that, when he shall appear, we shall be like him; for we shall see him as he is" (I John 3:2). Justification through faith in Christ's blood is the beginning, and being like Him when He appears is the consummation.

If our trials seem to be too great to bear, if what we are passing through seems to be greater than human flesh can stand, let us rest our hearts on this word from God: "For I reckon that the sufferings of this present time are not worthy to be compared with the glory that shall be revealed in us. . . . He that spared not his own Son, but delivered him up for us all, how shall he not with him also freely give us all things?" (Rom. 8:18,32).

Peter was also used of God to give us comfort with regard to the future: "Blessed be the God and Father of our Lord Jesus Christ, which according to his abundant mercy hath begotten us again unto a living hope by the resurrection of Jesus Christ from the dead, To an inheritance incorruptible, and undefiled, and that fadeth not away, reserved in heaven for you, Who are kept by the power of God through faith unto salvation ready to be revealed in the last time. Wherein ye greatly rejoice, though now for a season, if need be, ye are in heaviness through manifold temptations" (I Pet. 1:3-6).

Let us rest our minds on what the Lord Jesus said in Matthew 13: "The Son of man shall send forth his angels . . . Then shall the righteous shine forth as the sun in the kingdom of their Father" (v. 43).

Or think if you will with that grand old soldier of the cross, the Apostle Paul, as he neared the end of his earthly journey. Did he say in a discouraged or resigned manner: "This is the end"? Not at all! He triumphantly declared: "I have fought a good fight, I have finished my course, I have kept the faith: Henceforth there is laid up for me a crown of righteousness, which the Lord, the righteous judge, shall give me at that day: and not to me only, but unto all them also that love his appearing" (II Tim. 4:7,8).

> "Hark! a voice from Eden stealing,
>   Such as but to angels known,
> Hope its song of cheer is singing
>   'It is better farther on.'
>
> "Hope is singing, still is singing,
>   Softly in an undertone,
> Singing as if God had taught it,
>   'It is better farther on.'

"Night and day it sings the same song,
  Sings it when I sit alone;
Sings it so the heart may hear it,
  'It is better farther on.'

"On the grave it sits and sings it,
  Sings it when the heart would groan,
Sings it when the shadows darken,
  'It is better farther on.'

"Farther on! O how much farther?
  Count the milestones one by one;
No! not counting, only trusting,
  'It is better farther on.' "

One of the most meaningful Scriptures to me in this area of the worthwhileness of serving the Lord is Malachi 3:16-18: "Then they that feared the LORD spake often one to another: and the LORD hearkened, and heard it, and a book of remembrance was written before him for them that feared the LORD, and that thought upon his name. And they shall be mine, saith the LORD of hosts, in that day when I make up my jewels; and I will spare them, as a man spareth his own son that serveth him. Then shall ye return, and discern between the righteous and the wicked, between him that serveth God and him that serveth him not."

Let us not hold back from seeking to do the will of God. Let us not pretend to be right with God if we are not. Justification is obtained through faith, and the life that results from it is a life of faith expressed in willing obedience to the will of God. It is a life lived under the control of the Spirit of God.

Chapter Six

IF A MAN DIE WILL HE LIVE AGAIN?

The question of what follows death has occupied the minds of men as far back as we can trace history. The arguments and discussions surrounding this theme have often given off more heat than light. This is a theme concerning which men have written many books, but unaided human reason and experience have no answer.

Some persons have sought in many different ways to go behind the curtain that comes down at death to see what transpires, but it is all in vain. One man said to another as they viewed the body of a friend, "I wish I could talk with him now, for if he knows anything about what follows death, he knows more than we do."

A device that has been resorted to from time to time, one that goes back into the mists of antiquity, is that of seeking to contact the dead. Isaiah the prophet warned Israel in his day against this practice: "And when they shall say unto you, Seek unto them that have familiar spirits, and unto wizards that peep, and that mutter: should not a people seek unto their God? for the living to the dead? To the law and to the testimony: if they speak not according to this word, it is because there is no light in them" (Isa. 8:19,20).

Spiritism was widely practiced in the days of King Saul of Israel. He attempted to stamp out the practice but did not quite succeed. Then there came a moment in his own life when he wanted to communicate with Samuel who had been dead for some time. Saul sought out a sorceress living at Endor for this evil purpose (I Sam. 28).

Manasseh was the King of Judah, notorious for his use of enchantments, sorceries, divinations, and dealing with a familiar spirit (II Chron. 33:6). A familiar spirit was in reality a divining demon that would come readily at the call of the one possessed by it. Divination was the supposed art of gaining secret knowledge especially concerning the future. A ruler such as Manasseh who endorsed such practices gave protection and prestige to those evil persons in his kingdom who sought to communicate with the Devil and to look into the future.

The fact that men have tried by various means to see into the future, to tell what lies beyond our common sphere of knowledge is strong evidence of man's curiosity and even deep concern with the question: "If a man die, shall he live again?"

This is a matter that often haunts parents when death has visited the home. I have had fathers and mothers, heartbroken over the loss of a child, say to me: "Pastor, what is the condition of my child now? Will I ever see him again? Will I know him if I do see him?" These are questions that arise out of the central question Job asked.

Apparently Job began to compare the lot of man with that of some things he saw in nature. He considered man's life to be but of few days and full of trouble. He comes forth like a flower and is cut down. He flees as a shadow and does not continue to live (Job 14:1,2).

Then Job considered what happened to trees. He said, "For there is hope of a tree, if it be cut down, that it will sprout again, and that the tender branch thereof will not cease. Though the root thereof wax old in the earth, and the stock thereof die in the ground; Yet through the scent of water it will bud, and bring forth boughs like a plant. But man dieth, and wasteth away: yea, man giveth up the ghost, and where is he? As the waters fail from the sea, and the flood decayeth and drieth up; So man lieth down, and riseth not" (Job 14:7-12a).

Job was simply asking if man was not better than a tree? Perhaps we would never think of making such a comparison, but he did. In the New Testament our Lord made it plain that one man is worth more than the whole material world so far as God is concerned.

Do not think for a moment that Job was ignorant of the answer to this question. He was replying to Zophar's accusations that he, Job, was a sinner or else he would be serene, restful, safe and would be able to lie down and not be afraid. Job's answer was that if he sinned he would someday have to answer for his sin, he was not trying to hide anything. He argued, however, that a man is better than a tree. If a tree is cut down and will live again, surely a man who dies will also live again. In fact, in verse 14, where Job raises the question: "If a man die, shall he live again?" he also answers the question by saying, "All the days of my appointed time will I wait, till my change come. Thou shalt call, and I will answer to thee; thou wilt have a desire to the work of thine hands."

In the chapters following this, Job shows that he has faith in another life following this short earthly experience. And his expressions concerning it show it is to him something very real and sublime. For example, Bildad severely scolds Job saying, "How long will it be ere you make an end of words? mark, and afterwards we will speak" (18:2). In present-day language Bildad said to Job that he talked nonsense, he talked too much; if he would be quiet long enough, the others would be able to tell him something. Then Bildad subtly insinuated that Job was a wicked man and that because he was wicked he had terrors and had lost his children—his roots had dried up and his branches had been cut off, his name would be forgotten among men (vv. 16,17).

Job had an answer to this scathing attack upon him. He admitted that there were things that perplexed him. He said, "I cry out of wrong, but I am not heard: I cry aloud, but there is no judgment" (19:7). "He hath stripped me of my glory, and taken the crown from my head. He hath destroyed me on every side, and I am gone: and mine hope hath he removed like a tree" (vv. 9,10). "He hath put my brethren far from me, and mine acquaintance are verily estranged from me. My kinsfolk have failed, and my familiar friends have forgotten me. They that dwell in mine house, and my maids, count me for a stranger: I am an alien in their sight. I called my servant, and he gave me no answer; I intreated him with my mouth. My breath is strange to my wife, though I intreated for the children's sake of mine own body. Yea, young children despised me; I arose, and they spake against me. All my inward friends abhorred me: and they whom I loved are turned against me. My bone cleaveth to my skin and to my flesh, and I am escaped with the skin of my teeth" (vv. 13-20).

How would we answer in such a situation? If it seemed that God did not hear us and that everything was going wrong, what would be our reaction? Suppose we were stripped of all our material goods and our friends left us and our loved ones turned against us and we were broken in health—what would we think or say?

Job remembered two things that kept his life in balance under these difficult circumstances. He remembered that His redeemer was a living redeemer and that he, Job, would live again. Here are his words, "For I know that my redeemer liveth, and that he shall stand at the latter day upon the earth: And though after my skin worms destroy this body, yet in my flesh shall I see God: Whom I shall see for myself, and mine eyes shall behold, and not another; though my reins be consumed within me" (vv. 25-27).

In this Job anticipated Peter who wrote: "Blessed be the God and Father of our Lord Jesus Christ, which according to his abundant mercy hath begotten us again unto a lively hope by the resurrection of Jesus Christ from the dead, To an inheritance incorruptible, and undefiled, and that fadeth not away, reserved in heaven for you, Who are kept by the power of God through faith unto salvation ready to be revealed in the last time. Wherein ye greatly rejoice, though now for a season, if need be, ye are in heaviness through manifold temptations: That the trial of your faith, being much more precious than of gold that perisheth, though it be tried with fire, might be found unto praise and honour and glory at the appearing of Jesus Christ: Whom having not seen, ye love; in whom, though now ye see him not, yet believing, ye rejoice with joy unspeakable and full of glory: Receiving the end of your faith, even the salvation of your souls" (I Pet. 1:3-9).

Job is also a kinsman of Paul in the faith, and in his hope of the resurrection gives us a foretaste of I Corinthians 15 where Paul wrote: "For as in Adam all die, even so in Christ shall all be made alive. . . . The last enemy that shall be destroyed is death. . . . In a moment, in the twinkling of an eye, at the last trump: for the trumpet shall sound, and the dead shall be raised incorruptible, and we shall be changed. . . . Therefore, my beloved brethren, be ye stedfast, unmoveable, always abounding in the work of the Lord, forasmuch as ye know that your labour is not in vain in the Lord" (I Cor. 15: 22,26,52,58).

It is not all of life to live nor is it all of death to die. The Bible says that it is appointed unto men once to die, but after that there is judgment.

Our Saviour said in John 5:28,29: "Marvel not at this: for the hour is coming, in the which all that are in the graves shall hear his voice, And shall come forth; they that have done good, unto the resurrection of life; and they that have done evil, unto the resurrection of damnation." And centuries before these words were spoken, Isaiah said, "Thy dead men shall live, together with my dead body shall they arise. Awake and sing, ye that dwell in dust: for thy dew is as the dew of herbs, and the earth shall cast out the dead" (Isa. 26:19).

It was concerning judgment and resurrection that Paul ended his discourse on Mars Hill. "Because he hath appointed a day, in the which he will judge the world in righteousness by that man whom he hath ordained; whereof he hath given assurance to all men, in that he hath raised him from the dead" (Acts 17:31).

So it is no mystery that dead men shall live! They will live and think and feel and rejoice and weep. Many of them will stand ashamed before the bar of God's justice. They will confess their crimes to God with nothing held back. They will live to give an eye-witness account to every evil deed and every vile act they ever committed.

Is it any wonder that some hope the dead will not live again? But they will. We all will. Before God the truth will come out; all that the sinner ever thought was hidden will be known. All the rebellion of his heart that his fellowman might have considered cleverness on his part, all the ill-will of that day called strength of character, all the sin that was named self-expression, all the anger that was called righteous indignation—all of it shall stand condemned for what it actually was. Do we realize that in that day when men stand to be judged before God there will no longer be any unsolved robberies, no more unsolved murders? Everything will be known. The filthy talk, the life of adultery, covetousness, deceit, spite, yes every evil thing will be confessed by those guilty of such things. The very words of the unrighteous will condemn them. Daniel's words are arresting and full of dread for those involved where he said, "Many . . . shall awake . . . to shame and everlasting contempt" (12:2). How exposure of any fault leaves us embarrassed now. There is no telling to what length some of us will go to protect our name and our pride. But in that day, none of our self-protective devices will avail.

But there is another side to this picture. Some will live again to be like Jesus (I John 3:1). They will come into the full release of the pardon they accepted when Christ was made Lord of their lives. The glory of their eternity will be marked by the removal of the curse. They will see the face of God and His name shall be in their foreheads. They will live in everlasting light and reign with Christ forever and ever (see Rev. 21:22).

When death strikes at those who belong to the Lord, we should remember with new insight and assurance His words: "I am the resurrection, and the life: he that believeth in me, though he were dead, yet shall he live" (John 11:25).

There are three possible ways to die, and the way we die determines how we shall live. First of all we may die with Christ. This is the truth of Romans 6:6-11 where identification with Christ and His death and resurrection is the result of our placing our trust in Him as personal Saviour. It is this that opens to us all the treasures of salvation provided by God.

There is also death in Christ. It was this great truth that Paul used to bring comfort to the Thessalonian believers who wondered what would happen to their loved ones who had died and Christ had not returned. Paul showed them and also us how that those who die in Christ will be brought back with Him when He returns and will be given resurrection bodies. Those who belong to Christ and are alive at His coming will be caught up together with those who have died in Christ and will meet the Lord in the air and ever be with Him (I Thess. 4:13-18).

The third possibility, and this is one that God would have all men avoid, is dying without Christ. The consequences of this are brought before us in Revelation 20: 11-15 where the most solemn court scene in history will take place when the dead, small and great, stand before God and answer to Him for their rejection of Jesus Christ as Saviour and Lord.

> "Oh the way sometimes is low,
> And the waters dark and deep,
>   And I stumble as I go;
> But I have a tryst to keep,
> It was plighted long ago
>   With some who lie asleep.
> And tho days go dragging slow,
> And the sad hours gravewards creep,
> And the world is hushed in woe
>   I neither wail nor weep,
> For the Lord would not have it so,
>   I have a tryst to keep."

Chapter Seven

WHY DO THE WICKED PROSPER?

Job was a master at striking at the root of things. He could look at a problem and in very few words frame a question that went right to the heart of it. We face these same puzzles today, but sometimes we lack the ability to analyze the problems or we are reluctant to put our thoughts into words for fear we might be thought stupid.

Job's fifth question is one that every observing person has asked at one time or another. Philosophers, moralists and just plain everyday people have asked this question. Perhaps there have been times when we have shaken our heads in confusion and anger, and this query has boiled out of us in an angry outburst. Job put it in these words, "Wherefore do the wicked live, become old, yea, are mighty in power?" (Job 21:7). This is not an easy question to answer. It is too serious to be made light of. It cannot be passed off by a shrug of the shoulders. How many persons have remarked after observing the flourishing of the wicked: "It does not pay to be good. Others who have not tried half as hard as I have to do what is right are better off than I am."

Others have asked this same question down through the years. A great poet of another day wrote:

Blessed, almighty Jove!
With deep amazement I view the world, and marvel at
   your ways,
How can you reconcile it to your sense of right and
   wrong,
Thus loosely to dispense your bounties on the wick-
   ed and the good?
How can your laws be known or understood?

This man thought God was too loose with His blessings. It seemed that those who were wrong were blessed
and those who were right suffered. This was very much
Job's problem when he asked: "Wherefore do the wicked
live, become old, yea, are mighty in power?" (Job 21:7).

Some 450 years B.C. a great thinker by the name of
Euripides wrote: "Does someone say that there be gods
above? There are not, no, there are not, let no fool led
by old false fables, thus deceive you. Look at the facts
themselves, yielding my words no undue credence; for I
say that kings kill, rob, break oaths, lay cities waste by
fraud, and doing thus are happier than those who live
calm, pious lives day after day." To this man the prosperity of the wicked was an argument for atheism. There
just could not be a God or gods in heaven and this condition exist on earth.

Though Euripides could not reconcile the prosperity of
the wicked with the existence of a just God, he could not
find it in his heart to deny altogether that God existed.
He prayed, "O Zeus, if there be a Zeus, for I know him
only by report." It is obvious from this that the prosperity of the wicked is a knotty problem to any thinking person.

72

So far we have only seen one side of this puzzle, the side that deals with the seeming good treatment that evil men receive in this world. The other half of the problem is just as difficult to understand; Why does so much trouble and suffering fall upon the good? In his own mind Job was contrasting his own state of loss and suffering with that of wicked men whom he observed around him prosperous and in good health.

Not only did Job ask, "Wherefore do the wicked live, become old, yea, are mighty in power?" but he continued, "Their seed is established in their sight with them, and their offsprings before their eyes. Their houses are safe from fear, neither is the rod of God upon them" (vv. 8,9). Remember that part of Job's loss was the loss of his children. A great wind had destroyed the house in which his sons and daughters were eating. Job's family was wiped out in that one terrible storm.

Whereas Job had lost his flocks and herds the wicked were prospering. "Their bull gendereth," Job said, "and faileth not; their cow calveth, and casteth not her calf" (v. 10). Cattle then as now provided much of the living for people. There was milk for food, power for plowing and meat for the table.

Job was not the only one who saw this seeming disparity. The wicked themselves saw it and reacted in accordance with their evil hearts. Job said of it, "They send forth their little ones like a flock, and their children dance. They take the timbrel and harp, and rejoice at the sound of the organ. They spend their days in wealth, and in a moment go down to the grave. Therefore they say unto God, Depart from us; for we desire not the knowledge of thy ways. What is the Almighty, that we should serve him? and what profit should we have, if we pray unto him?" (21:11-15). The wicked also saw that the righteous often suffer while those living in evil go free. They concluded then that they did not need to pray, nor seek God, nor walk in His ways, nor serve Him. They just wanted Him to leave them alone. They believed that they were far better off than those who tried to observe these matters.

Job was a good example of the righteous suffering adversities. He was trying his best to be good and obedient before God. He was trying to walk in his ways and to serve Him acceptably. He was one who "rose up early in the morning, and offered burnt-offerings according to the number of (his children)."

When speaking to the Devil concerning Job, the Lord said, "Hast thou considered my servant Job, that there is none like him in the earth, a perfect and an upright man, one that feareth God, and escheweth (avoids) evil?" Yet calamity fell upon Job and he could not escape it. Job's problem had to do with the fact that he was a man seeking to walk in the will of God but was stripped of all means of making a living and of his family and of his health. The problem is still with us!

John Bunyan in his famous Christian allegory, *Pilgrims Progress*, sought to answer this same puzzle. "Christian," the main character, had one struggle after another as he walked the right road, while those who abandoned themselves to folly and pleasure enjoyed unbroken ease!

What we think we see as we observe these things is

74

that we are creatures or victims of the unaccountable wheel of fortune or chance. There seems to be no rhyme or reason for the things that happen to us. Our conflict of mind and heart comes when we attempt to reconcile the misfortunes of good men and seemingly good fortunes of bad men with the justice and wisdom of God.

Bible Writers Comment on This Puzzle

Solomon, famed for his wisdom and noted for his keen observations saw this very thing and said, "There is a vanity which is done upon the earth; that there be just men, unto whom it happeneth according to the work of the wicked; again, there be wicked men, to whom it happeneth according to the work of the righteous: I said that this also is vanity. Then I commendeth mirth, because a man hath no better thing under the sun, than to eat, and to drink, and to be merry; for that shall abide with him of his labour the days of his life, which God giveth him under the sun" (Eccles. 8:14,15).

Another of the writers of Scripture who commented on this was Asaph, author of a number of the Psalms. One of them, Psalm 73, takes up this very subject. Asaph sang, "Truly God is good to Israel, even to such as are of a clean heart." He knew this to be true, but it was not what he had observed with his eyes, for he went on to say, "But as for me, my feet were almost gone; my steps had well nigh slipped." Here is the reason: "For I was envious at the foolish, when I saw the prosperity of the wicked." Asaph could not make the puzzle go together. How was it that the wicked would prosper and the good not?

He continued with his observation, "For there are no

bands in their (the wicked's) death: but their strength is firm." This is a cause for real wonder, for surely if there is a real difference between the righteous and the wicked, it will show up at the time of their death. The notion that is common among us and one hard to get rid of is that a quiet death means a happy hereafter. But a quiet death may simply be the result of a hard heart. Some men are so foolish as to play games with their hearts until they are so hard that when death comes, they continue to ignore God even at that critical time.

Asaph continued his song concerning the wicked: "They are not in trouble as other men . . . Therefore pride compasseth (surrounds) them as a chain; violence covereth them as a garment. Their eyes stand out with fatness: they have more than heart could wish. They are corrupt, and speak wickedly concerning oppression: they speak loftily. They set their mouth against the heavens, and their tongue walketh through the earth. Therefore his people return hither: and waters of a full cup are wrung out to them." What Asaph is saying here is that these wicked persons offer a full cup to any who will join with them in their evil ways, those who will have a good time and not be party spoilers.

"How doth God know? and is there knowledge in the most High? Behold, these are the ungodly, who prosper in the world; they increase in riches. Verily I have cleansed my heart in vain, and washed my hands in innocency. For all the day long have I been plagued, and chastened every morning. If I say, I will speak thus; behold, I should offend against the generation of thy children. When I thought to know this, it was too painful for me." This was too much for Asaph to reason out without the help of God.

Jeremiah was also plagued by this same puzzle for he wrote: "Righteous art thou, O Lord, when I plead with thee: yet let me talk with thee of thy judgments: Wherefore doth the way of the wicked prosper? wherefore are all they happy that deal very treacherously? Thou hast planted them, yea, they have taken root: they grow, yea, they bring forth fruit: thou art near in their mouth, and far from their reins. But thou, O Lord, knowest me: thou has seen me, and tried mine heart . . ." (Jer. 12:1-3).

Habakkuk was another prophet of God who was plagued by this question. He saw the sins of his people and was perplexed by God's seeming silence. Here is what he wrote about the matter: "Art thou not from everlasting, O Lord my God, mine Holy One? we shall not die. O Lord, thou hast ordained them for judgment; and, O mighty God, thou hast established them for correction. Thou art of purer eyes than to behold evil, and canst not look on iniquity: wherefore lookest thou upon them that deal treacherously, and holdest thy tongue when the wicked devoureth the man that is more righteous than he? And makest men as the fishes of the sea, as the creeping things, that have no ruler over them? They take up all of them with the angle, they catch them in their net, and gather them in their drag: therefore they rejoice and are glad. Therefore they sacrifice unto their net, and burn incense unto their drag; because by them their portion is fat, and their meat plenteous. Shall they therefore empty their net, and not spare continually to slay the nations?" (Hab. 1:12-17).

It is the nature of human beings to ask questions, yet I think ours is a generation that is asking more questions than any other. We want to know the why of just about everything. We start life like a lookout on a boat that is lost. We never know what is ahead. We have to ask questions in the hope that we will learn what is coming.

Some questions are childish and others are very simple to answer. Children want to know where the light goes when the lamp is turned off. They want to know where the sun disappears to and why it does not burn up. But as we grow older, we want the answers to some of the more complicated and serious things of life. And there comes a day, when, like Job, we face the question of why it is that the innocent often suffer and the wicked often seem to be blessed. Some of life's questions appear to be unanswerable. They are problems that seemingly cannot be solved. We are puzzled by what happens to us and what happens to those about us.

"Why did this happen to me?" is one of the most common questions any of us ask. "Why am I sick?" "Why am I poor?" "Why are some rich who make no attempt to do the right things?" "Why was our child taken when he was such a good child?" What pastor has not faced this question uttered by broken-hearted parents?

Some people try very hard to be what they should be. The father leads his family in devotions to God. He sees that they have every advantage possible to grow spiritually and to live morally right in this world. Yet, trouble seems to hound them as a bloodhound follows the course of an escaped convict. The wife and mother may become ill, and the children get into one trouble after another.

Work may fail, and finally the man himself may die in agony from some dread disease.

In contrast there are those of whom we could correctly say, "God is not in all their thoughts." They live entirely for themselves. They take every selfish advantage to gain their ends and do not care at whose expense they gain their goals. They eat their food and never once thank God for it nor for the ability to taste and enjoy it. They heedlessly use God's name in vain. They are smug and shameless, yet they are successful in business. Troubles that plague the ordinary person never seem to come near them. As Job said, their houses are safe from fear, neither is the rod of God upon them. . . . They send forth their little ones like a flock, and their children dance. They take the timbrel and the harp and rejoice at the sound of the organ (Job 21:9-12).

This puzzle reaches its climax in the person and life of Jesus Christ himself. His was the mind that planned the world: "All things were made by him and without him was not anything made that was made." It was His purpose that this world should be a good world (Gen. 1:31). His thoughts as He walked among men were pure and undefiled. He spoke words that blessed the people of His day and all the ages since. But wicked men crowned His head with thorns and lived to boast about it. His were the hands which held the thunderbolts of heaven, yet rested in blessing upon children on city streets. Cruel men took His hands and spiked them to a tree and lived to laugh at Him.

Jesus Christ had walked the eternal pathways. While on earth His feet took Him only on missions of mercy.

Yet cruel men made His feet fast with nails driven in by a Roman mall and lived to mock Him. How could this be? Why did God stand by and let this take place? Why did He not burn the world to a crisp from the heat of the sun? Why did He not turn the winds loose and blow these wicked men off into space leaving them to fall forever? It seemed that for a season the wicked triumphed, accomplished their diabolical purposes, laughed and went their way!

We must face this problem and seek an answer. We make no claim to have all the answers for every situation. It has often been my lot to sit beside the bed of the dying and say, "I don't know why this must be." This has taught me not to try to explain every event in life.

Some Answers to the Puzzle

Let us look again at our puzzle. What is it we are seeking an answer for? It is this: Why does God allow the wicked to live on in their wickedness? Why is it so many persons are getting by with so much evil?

The first answer I would suggest is the Scriptures teach us that God allows the wicked to live in order that they might turn to Him. God wants to make miracles of mercy of them, to give them life so that they might be transformed by His grace into the sons of God. We so easily forget that each one of us who is saved was saved by grace alone and not because we were so good that the Lord was forced to take us in. Jesus said, "I am not come to call the righteous, but sinners to repentance" (Matt. 9:13).

We sometimes think that we are better than others. We

forget that were it not for the grace of God we would all perish (Luke 13:3). God does not force salvation upon us, but waits for us to repent, to admit that we are sinners in need. It is then that He can take the greatest of sinners and make them His children through faith in Christ Jesus.

We read in the Word of God that He would "have all men to be saved, and to come unto the knowledge of the truth" (I Tim. 2:4). It would be hard for some people to believe the kind of lives some of God's servants led before they were converted to Jesus Christ. They did not become ministers of the gospel because they were saintly. They were sinners by nature and by grace were saved. Then God laid upon them the burden of telling this wonderful grace to others. We do not say this to magnify anyone's former sinful life, but to magnify the grace of our God.

It was the lost sinner that Jesus came to seek and save. Peter, a cursing fisherman, became the mighty preacher at Pentecost. Saul, the persecutor of the Christians, became the great Apostle of Christ to the Gentiles. Through his life and through the inspired epistles he wrote, he was instrumental in changing more lives than perhaps any other servant of Christ who has ever lived.

These are but a sample of the great host who have become members of God's family through faith in Christ Jesus. These feel kin to Paul when he said that he was the chiefest of sinners. With one voice we thank God for letting us live to come to know what it means to be saved from our sins through the redemption in Christ.

To you who read this and who are not yet trusting in Christ, there is hope for you while there is life. Why not heed the call of Christ. Come as you are and receive Him by faith as your Saviour. You, too, will know the joy of sins forgiven.

> "The mercy of God is an ocean divine,
> A boundless, fathomless flood.
> Launch out into the deep, cut away the
>   shore line
> And be lost in the fullness of God."

So then, God allows the wicked to live in order that they might repent and be saved from their sin. It is always good for us to remember that "God commendeth his love toward us, in that, while we were yet sinners, Christ died for us" (Rom. 5:8).

God does not allow the wicked to live so that they may go on in their wickedness and sneer at God's people. The unsaved should not use their time to boast of their strength and their own plans and ignore the things of the Lord. They are allowed to live only that they might make good use of that time to come to Christ. Never is life and time granted in order that any of us might go through life with utter disregard for righteousness. The appeal in the Word is for us to "come." Now is the day of salvation. Our strength, our opportunities, our ability to think—all of these things will go some day, so let us use them to make the right decision now.

Job not only wondered why the wicked were allowed to continue on in their wickedness, but he was puzzled by the fact that they were often blest abundantly in material ways. Why should this be? God answers that for us when He says in Romans 2:4: "Or despisest thou the riches of his goodness and forbearance and longsuffering; not knowing that the goodness of God leadeth thee to repentance?" God sometimes takes the sinner and treats him as a father might treat a wayward son, giving him more attention than he would other children simply in order to break the son's heart by the father's goodness. So it is that God pours out His loving-kindness to sinners. He seeks to humble their hearts in order that they will turn to Him in complete trust.

We sometimes think that God is slow in keeping His promise of final retribution and wrath upon the wicked. Peter disclosed the real purpose of God in withholding judgment. He wrote, "The Lord is not slack concerning his promise, as some men count slackness; but is longsuffering to us-ward, not willing that any should perish, but that all should come to repentance" (II Pet. 3:9). Time is given us to use for eternity. God's blessings are poured upon us in order to bring us to repentance.

There are always two sides, however, to every coin. We are inclined to forget that the Scriptures tell us that the way of the wicked is hard. Somewhere, sometime, things must and will be made right. God allows the prosperity of the wicked in order to show that there must be a judgment to come. The injustices of the world are not always made right in this life. It is not all of life to live, nor all of death to die.

We recall with horror some of the crimes that took place in the last World War. It is true that some of the criminals were apprehended, but not all. And who can say that the judgment men meted out was sufficient for the horrible crimes committed.

We cannot always evaluate motive any more than we can ever evaluate the far-reaching effects of a crime. A man may in a sudden rage kill another who is the head of a family. Society punishes the killer for the crime of murder, but who can measure the grief of the widow, or who can weigh the anguish in the hearts of the children because they are fatherless? Or who can spell out the bitterness such loss may cause these children as they grow up. Somewhere justice must be measured out to suit the crime in an exact way.

What about little children who suffer, weep, starve and die because men like mad monsters fight and destroy? Someone has been quoted as saying that such and such a crime took place on last Tuesday and God did not even notice. But someone has answered saying, "Yes, but do not forget that God does not pay all of His bills on Tuesday!" Somewhere, sometime, God will make all things right. We forget so easily that all must appear before God, there to receive just dues for the things done in the body.

We may often exclaim: "Look what he is getting by with!" Remember, whatever "he" is getting by with, is only for a time. We read in Acts 17:31: God "hath appointed a day, in the which he will judge the world in righteousness by that man whom he hath ordained; whereof he hath given assurance unto all men, in that he hath raised him from the dead."

In Proverbs 11 we read: "Though hand join in hand, the wicked shall not go unpunished." The wicked may

84

live and prosper, but the end is not yet, for judgment will come.

Do not overlook the fact that Job, Solomon, Asaph and Jeremiah had an answer to this question of why the wicked are allowed to live and prosper. While none of these men could understand all the ways of the Lord, they trusted Him for what they could not understand. This is the kind of trust that all the children of God may have.

"I cannot understand
The why and wherefore of a thousand things:
The drosses, the annoyances, the daily stings,
   I cannot understand,
   But I can trust
For perfect trusting perfect comfort brings.

"I cannot see the end,
The hidden meaning of each trial sent,
The pattern into which each tangled thread is lent,
   I cannot see the end,
   But I can trust,
And in God's changless love I am content."

A Time of Reckoning

Job remembered that "the wicked is reserved to the day of destruction? they shall be brought forth to the day of wrath" (Job 21:30). Solomon had much to say about this same subject. In the instructions to his son he said, "The curse of the LORD is in the house of the wicked: but he blesseth the habitation of the just. Surely he scorneth the scorners: but he giveth grace unto the lowly. The wise shall inherit glory: but shame shall be the

85

promotion of fools" (Prov. 3:33-35). "The memory of the just is blessed: but the name of the wicked shall rot" (Prov. 10:7).

We have seen how Asaph in Psalm 73 was puzzled over the prosperity of the wicked. He could not find an answer to his problem until, he said, "I went into the sanctuary of God; then understood I their end." He got his thoughts straight when he began to think as God thinks. He had to see things from the sanctuary, that is from the viewpoint of God. Such a perspective is what we need. We are shortsighted; we are impatient; we see through a darkened glass.

After seeing things from God's viewpoint Asaph's song changes: "Surely thou didst set them in slippery places: thou castedst them down into destruction. How are they brought into desolation, as in a moment! they are utterly consumed with terrors. . . . Thou shalt guide me with thy counsel, and afterward receive me to glory!"

Think with Jeremiah when he turned to those who prospered in wickedness and were happy only when they dealt in treachery. He asked the question that all such might well ponder: "How wilt thou do in the swelling of Jordan?" (Jer. 12:5). Indeed, where will the wicked flee when the deep waters roll? There will come a time when the grace of God will no longer be available. There will be none to turn to when death overtakes us, and we are still rejecting God's offer.

We are all here for a brief season. Now is the time to come to the Saviour. This is the accepted time. It is today that the invitation goes out. "Come unto me," our Saviour said, "all ye that labour and are heavy laden, and I will give you rest. Take my yoke upon you, and learn of me; for I am meek and lowly in heart: and ye shall find rest unto your souls" (Matt. 11:28,29).

"O turn ye, O turn ye, for why will ye die,
When God in great mercy is coming so nigh?
Now Jesus invites you, the Spirit says, 'Come,'
And angels are waiting to welcome you home.

"And now Christ is ready your souls to receive,
O how can you question, if you will believe?
If sin is your burden, why will you not come?
'Tis you He bids welcome; He bids you come home.

"In riches, in pleasures, what can you obtain
To sooth your affliction, or banish your pain?
To bear up your spirit when summoned to die,
Or waft you to mansions of glory on high?

"Why will you be starving, and feeding on air?
There's mercy in Jesus, enough and to spare;
If still you are doubting, make trial and see
And prove that His mercy is boundless and free."

Let no one deceive you concerning the fact that Jesus Christ is able to save you now. He died for the ungodly. Put your trust in Him and rest in His finished work for you.

Neither be deceived into thinking that there is escape from sin and its consequences outside of Christ. The warning of Scripture is, "How shall we escape, if we neglect so great salvation. . . ." (Heb. 2:3). God will judge sin at one of two places: either at Calvary where Jesus paid the penalty, or at the Great White Throne

Judgment where the sinner pays the penalty. God's invitation is still open, however: "Behold, I stand at the door, and knock: if any man hear my voice, and open the door, I will come in to him, and will sup with him, and he with me" (Rev. 3:20).

Another answer to our questions as to why the wicked live and become old and are mighty in power is that love does not need the answers to all questions that come along. Neither does love need to answer all such questions. There are many things that a child cannot understand about the things his father does, but because he loves and trusts his father, he does what he is told. So it is with us and our Heavenly Father.

We cannot understand for the present, at least, all the things He does. But we know that He knows what He is doing, and because we love and trust Him we let the matter rest there. Quite often we do not understand why things should be as they are, but we know His way is best and wait until He sees fit to shed more light on the things that perplex us. Neither should we try to find an answer to those who may ask us, "Why did God let this happen to me?" We know God has the answer, and that is sufficient for us.

We often grow impatient and demand that circumstances should be worked out according to our plans and that right now. In this we overlook the fact that we are not the only persons in the world who are suffering. Perhaps we recall reading of the man who said, "I was miserable because I had no shoes, until I met a man who had no feet!" It is easy to so concentrate on our own sorrows that we cannot see the sorrow of others. We tend to forget that if we know nothing of trials ourselves, we will not be able to help others in similar circumstances. To whom does a mother who has just lost her child go for comfort? To another mother who has had a similar sorrow, for with her there will not only be sympathy, but understanding also.

Toward the end of the Book of Job we find that the patriarch prayed for his friends. Could he have prayed with deep compassion if he himself had not suffered greatly? Often our trials and sorrows are blessings in disguise. God allows them to come to us so that we may be of service to others who experience similar difficulties. When in need of comfort, all of us find that there is no one who can help us like the person who can honestly say, "I know how you feel, for I went through that same thing myself!"

If we are willing to look away unto Jesus and, therefore, away from ourselves, we will become a greater blessing than we ever dreamed was possible. The purpose of our sufferings may be so that we can minister to others. Deep calls unto deep. The heart that is broken knows the heart that is breaking. It was for this reason that our Saviour warned His disciples against seeking authority or a high place in life, but suggested instead, "Whosoever will be great among you, let him be your minister; And whosoever will be chief among you, let him be your servant: Even as the Son of man came not to be ministered unto, but to minister, and to give his life a ransom for many" (Matt. 20:26-28). As He pointed out in another place, the way to save our life is to lose it. Even though from the human standpoint we might think we have reason to complain or be despondent or bitter and even rebellious, the truth is that there is no justification for any of these. If we lose our life in service for Jesus' sake, we will save it as He said (Matt. 16:25).

Some Benefits to the Sufferer

It has been well said that all sunshine and nothing else makes a desert. This is true on the earth and it is also true in the heart. No field produces like the field that has been plowed up. No one can really sing the songs of a broken heart unless he has had a broken heart. None can weep with those who weep unless they too have known the taste of tears. The sweetest perfume comes from the flower that has been crushed. Sorrow, broken hearts, tired lives, disappointed hopes—these are topics of all time, but they are understood only by those who have experienced them.

> "I walked a mile with pleasure,
> She chattered all the way,
> But not a thing she taught me,
> With all she had to say.
>
> "I walked a mile with sorrow,
> And not a word said she,
> But O, the things she taught me,
> When sorrow walked with me."

A man of God once said to me, "If I must choose between being healthy and being holy, I choose to be holy." Someone in deep trouble wrote: "Amid my list of blessings infinite, stands this the foremost, that my heart has bled."

"If, as I live, I could become
  Immune to beauty's call
And never be affected
  By a lovely rose at all;
If I could watch a sunset
  And not become inspired
Nor by a burning bush
  That autumn flame has fired;
Or have a friend to play me false
  And never shed a tear,
And to another friend in pain
  I'd turn a deafened ear
I'm sure, then, I'd suffer less
  If all of this were so;
But, if it were, I'd just as well
  Have died long years ago."

This was the very character of our Lord's life among us. "Forasmuch then as the children are partakers of flesh and blood, he also himself likewise took part of the same; that through death he might destroy him that had the power of death, that is, the devil; And deliver them who through fear of death were all their lifetime subject to bondage. For verily he took not on him the nature of angels; but he took on him the seed of Abraham. Wherefore in all things it behoved him to be made like unto his brethren, that he might be a merciful and faithful high priest in things pertaining to God, to make reconciliation for the sins of the people. For in that he himself hath suffered being tempted, he is able to succour them that are tempted" (Heb. 2:14-18).

This was the truth Paul gave to the believers in Corinth: "Blessed be God, even the Father of our Lord Jesus Christ, the Father of mercies, and the God of all comfort; Who comforteth us in all our tribulation, that we may be able to comfort them which are in any trouble, by the comfort wherewith we ourselves are comforted of God" (II Cor. 1:3,4).

Later on in the same book where Paul refers to a disciplinary action he had the church in Corinth take in regard to one of its members, he wrote: "Nevertheless God, that comforteth those that are cast down, comforted us by the coming of Titus. . . . Wherefore, though I wrote unto you, I did it not for his cause that had done the wrong, nor for his cause that suffered wrong, but that our care for you in the sight of God might appear unto you. Therefore we were comforted in your comfort: yea, and exceedingly the more joyed we for the joy of Titus, because his spirit was refreshed by you all" (II Cor. 7: 6,12,13).

> "If none were sick and none were sad,
>   What service could we render?
> I think if we were always glad,
>   We scarcely could be tender.
>
> "Did our beloved never need
>   Our patient ministration,
> Earth would grow cold, and miss, indeed,
>   Its sweetest consolation.
>
> "If sorrow never claimed our heart,
>   And every wish were granted,
> Patience would die, and
>   Life would be disenchanted."

While we may not understand why it is we suffer at the very time we are trying to do our best, and at a time when evildoers are getting by with so much, let us remember this: The world is filled with troubled hearts who need a word of comfort. They may be waiting for that word that we alone can give.

> "So the heart from the hardest trial
>   Gains the purest joy of all,
> And from lips that have tasted sadness,
>   The sweetest songs will fall.
> For as peace comes after suffering,
>   And love is reward of pain,
> So after earth comes heaven,
>   And out of our loss the gain!"

Let us not fail to point the sorrowing to the Man of Sorrows; or the disappointed to Him who never disappoints; or the bruised to Him who was bruised for our iniquities; or the comfortless to Him who knows the longing of every heart.

Another thing to consider when we think of the prosperity of the wicked and the suffering of the good is that we readily see the things that we want to see. Remember, Job did not say that all the righteous suffer and that all the wicked are prosperous; but when we are suffering, we tend to look at life in that way. The fact is that many who are righteous are prosperous, and many who are wicked suffer terribly. The person who looks at a few isolated cases only and then complains that it does not pay to be good is not being wise. He is acting like the Psalmist who said at one time in his haste: "All men are liars" (Ps. 116:11).

Advantages of Good Homes

All the good things in life cannot be measured by money. It may yet be true that the best things in life are free. There is a great advantage from being born into a righteous home. What a rich heritage those have whose parents sing the hymns and songs that mold the child into a right relationship with God. Think of the love, the devotion, the spiritual influence that such children receive right from the moment of birth. It has often been said that the hand that rocks the cradle rules the world. What a privilege to have that hand belong to a mother who walks with God. Oh, mother, what a responsibility is yours when you cradle that little life in your arm, and hug it to your bosom with unspeakable joy!

There are advantages received by being trained in the home of righteous parents. Think of the training that comes from a righteous father who says, "My son, attend to my words; incline thine ear unto my sayings. Let them not depart from thine eyes; keep them in the midst of thine heart. For they are life unto those that find them, and health to all their flesh. Keep thy heart with all diligence; for out of it are the issues of life. Put away from thee a froward mouth, and perverse lips put far from thee. Let thine eyes look right on, and let thine eyelids look straight before thee. Ponder the path of thy feet, and let all thy ways be established. Turn not to the right hand nor to the left: remove thy foot from evil" (Prov. 4:20-27).

Think of what it means to be taught to watch with care our speech and our actions, to ponder the direction our life is taking and to learn to walk righteously. Think of the advantage of being trained to hate what God hates. We need a revival of the teaching of the things God says He hates such as pride, lying, injustice, wicked plots, hurting others, telling lies about others and making trouble among brethren (Prov. 6:16-19).

Do we as fathers and mothers care about these matters? Do we take time to talk to our children concerning them, can we take them aside and talk to them calmly and naturally about such subjects as God, sin, salvation and righteous living?

Think of the distinct advantage of being trained to know wisdom, justice and judgment. What a blessing to have a foundation laid for the love of sobriety and for the hating of foolishness, to love the counsel of the Lord, to forsake not mercy and truth, and to honor the Lord with our substance. How good it is to understand early in life the chastening of the Lord and not to be weary of His correction: "For whom the Lord loveth he correcteth, even as a father the son in whom he delighteth."

For us to learn to turn to God when we are corrected and not against Him is an invaluable lesson to us. For us to have our own way generally leads to despair and darkness. But in following the Lord's way we find that wisdom is of more value than silver or gold or precious stones. True wisdom is true riches and honor.

Think also of the advantage of being taught to honor father and mother as the Lord has commanded. Some children have lost some of the best things in life because they were not taught by word of lip and deed of life to honor their parents. It is the wise son who makes a glad father; but a foolish son is the heaviness of his mother

(Prov. 10:1). Sorry indeed is the lot of the son who thinks of his mother as the one who nags and his father as "the old man" because they seek to have him walk in the ways of the Lord.

A great influence for good is brought to bear upon us if we are raised in an environment of righteousness. Do not shout too quickly that it does not pay to be righteous. The kind of language we hear about us every day influences us in a very marked manner. If what we hear is swearing, vulgar speech and suggestive talk, it will take a miracle of God's grace to undo the effect of it in our hearts.

Think of the influence of kindness expressed by each member in the home, honesty in dealing, gentleness in disposition, a home where the effort is made to live as Christians should. But if in the home we cheat or are sour in disposition or cruel with our tongues and unkind to one another, we will reap what we sow.

Think also of the peace of heart that is the reward of living righteously. "The LORD will give strength unto his people; the LORD will bless his people with peace" (Ps. 29:11). Contrast this with Isaiah 57:20,21: "But the wicked are like the troubled sea, when it cannot rest, whose waters cast up mire and dirt. There is no peace, saith my God, to the wicked." The knowledge of peace alone is worth all the effort that we may extend in living for God.

Consider some of the Scripture passages with regard to peace. "For he is our peace" (Eph. 2:14). "Being justified by faith, we have peace with God through our Lord Jesus Christ" (Rom. 5:1). "To be spiritually minded is life and peace" (Rom. 8:6). "For the kingdom of God is not meat and drink; but righteousness, and peace, and joy in the Holy Ghost" (Rom. 14:17). "But the meek shall inherit the earth; and shall delight themselves in the abundance of peace" (Ps. 37:11). "Great peace have they which love thy law: and nothing shall offend them" (Ps. 119:165). "The fruit of the Spirit is . . . peace" (Gal. 5:22). "Be careful (anxious) for nothing; but in every thing by prayer and supplication with thanksgiving let your requests be made known unto God. And the peace of God, which passeth all understanding, shall keep your hearts and minds through Christ Jesus. Finally, brethren, whatsoever things are true, honest, just, pure, of good report . . . think on these things . . . and the God of peace shall be with you" (Phil. 4:6-9).

The person was correct who wrote:

"It pays to serve Jesus, it pays every day,
It pays every step of the way!"

It is not enough, however, to merely consider the value of a righteous life over the brief span we live of some sixty or seventy years. Of course, if we are but creatures of clay, chance comers to this world, muddling around for a time and then turning back to the clods, then we may live like clods and forget this whole business of righteous living. But that is not all there is to life. Man was made a living soul, and he will exist forever and ever— somewhere. So it is well not only to consider that it pays to serve God and walk with Him, but it makes a difference in the way we die if we walk righteously. Paul has written, "For I reckon that the sufferings of this present time are not worthy to be compared with the glory which shall be revealed in us" (Rom. 8:18).

With regard to the wicked, the Scriptures state: "Like sheep they are laid in the grave; death shall feed on them; and the upright shall have dominion over them in the morning; and their beauty shall consume in the grave from their dwelling" (Ps. 49:14). There is a marked contrast in the death of the righteous: "Precious in the sight of the LORD is the death of his saints" (Ps. 116:15). "Mark the perfect man, and behold the upright: for the end of that man is peace" (Ps. 37:37). "The wicked is driven away in his wickedness: but the righteous hath hope in his death" (Prov. 14:32). The Prophet Balaam, when he beheld Israel, said, "Let me die the death of the righteous, and let my last end be like his!" (Num. 23:10). But to die the death of the righteous one must first live the life of the righteous.

But the end is not yet! Death leads to judgment, for "It is appointed unto men once to die, but after this the judgment" (Heb. 9:27). When we stand before God do you think that it would be a matter of sorrow to us that we have lived righteously for our Saviour? Indeed not!

James wrote: "Grudge not one against another, brethren, lest ye be condemned: behold, the judge standeth before the door" (James 5:9). Remember this and walk in righteousness! And with that recall the advice of Solomon to young men: "Rejoice, O young man, in thy youth; and let thy heart cheer thee in the days of thy youth, and walk in the ways of thine heart, and in the sight of thine eyes: but know thou, that for all these things God will bring thee into judgment. Therefore remove sorrow from thy heart, and put away evil from thy flesh: for childhood and youth are vanity" (Eccles. 11:9,10).

The end of all things is at hand; therefore, we must be sober and watch unto prayer.

Chapter Eight

WHERE IS WISDOM TO BE FOUND?

We consider another of Job's puzzles. This is the sixth, though it is not the sixth question Job asks in the book bearing his name. We have selected this one because it represents a problem faced not only by Job but by men in all ages.

At first glance this question may seem very simple. Job asked, "Where shall wisdom be found? and where is the place of understanding?" (28:12). Like so many other things, however, that seem easy at first, we may find it difficult to find the correct answer.

The search for wisdom has been the "holy grail" that some men have sought for all their lives. Many have failed to find it because they looked in the wrong place.

How our generation tries to be wise! Wisdom is defined as the power to judge rightly and follow the soundest course of action based on knowledge, experience and understanding. It is easy to see why wisdom is so precious and why Job would ask where it was to be found. There is so little of it at any time.

Wisdom is supposed to be possessed by the aged, for they have had time to assimilate and analyze what the experiences of life have taught. In line with this we name the teeth we get last our "wisdom teeth." Our third molars usually appear when we are between the ages of 17 and 25. So, when youth speaks up, the older ones respond: "What does he know? He has not even cut his wisdom teeth!"

One need not look hard to observe that a man can be foolish, even though he is old. There is a saying among us to the effect that "there is no fool like an old fool." No, wisdom does not come to us merely because we grow older. At the same time, it is not found with the young simply because they are young.

In thinking on this subject Job mentions several places where wisdom will not be found. He says, "Man knoweth not the price thereof; neither is it found in the land of the living" (28:13). The patriarch is saying in effect that man does not possess wisdom by himself. Job continued, "The depth saith, It is not in me: and the sea saith, It is not with me. It cannot be gotten for gold, neither shall silver be weighed for the price thereof. It cannot be valued with the gold of Ophir, with the precious onyx, or the sapphire. The gold and the crystal cannot equal it: and the exchange of it shall not be for jewels of fine gold. No mention shall be made of coral, or of pearls: for the price of wisdom is above rubies. The topaz of Ethiopia shall not equal it, neither shall it be valued with pure gold" (vv. 14-19). In other words, no amount of wealth can buy wisdom. To be rich does not mean to be wise.

Wisdom's Source

"Whence then cometh wisdom?" asked Job. "And where is the place of understanding?" (v. 20). This was not a problem without a solution. Job not only asked the question but he reached a conclusion. His reason, his experience and above all, his faith, led him straight to the point: "God understandeth the way thereof, and he knoweth the place thereof. . . . He prepared it, yea, and searched it out. And unto man he said, Behold, the fear of the Lord, that is wisdom; and to depart from evil is understanding" (vv. 23,27,28). True wisdom starts in the cradle and not in the college classroom. It starts first in the heart of man through wise teaching from the Scriptures at home. It starts with worship of God, not with the wise sayings of men.

If we know the answer, why is wisdom so hard to find? The reason is spiritual and moral. Wisdom cannot be found by the selfish heart. Our judgment is largely of a selfish nature, based on what we want, what we think, and how we feel. In fact, we often think with our emotions. This is why we sometimes pass off what we consider bad judgment on the part of another by saying, "Don't pay any attention to him, he is not feeling well today." We recognize the truth that we seldom speak wisdom, for all too often we express our feelings which cannot be trusted in most cases. When we are led by our feelings we are in constant hot water.

When we look for a man to be a judge among us, we try to choose one who can judge rightly, that is as much as a human being can. We look for a man with experience and sound judgment, a man who is willing to lay aside his personal feelings and stick to the facts in a given case. Sound judgment is such a difficult matter to most of us that we have another humorous statement with a great deal of truth in it: "I have made up my mind, so you need not try to confuse me with facts."

The Bible says, "All we like sheep have gone astray; we have turned every one to his own way" (Isa. 53:6). That is why it is hard to be wise. We find it easier to go our way than God's way. This was Adam's sin and it is ours. We refuse to surrender to God. We would rather go our own way and die than go His way and live.

Another reason why wisdom is hard to find is that it is costly. We have already seen that Job estimated its value to be far above material things and the writer of the Proverbs does likewise. He said, "Wisdom is better than rubies; and all the things that may be desired are not to be compared to it" (Prov. 8:11).

Let us not for a moment confuse wisdom with cleverness or wittiness. Many of our attempts to show cleverness are but cover-ups for our stupidity. People who make a habit of this are sometimes known among us as "smart alecks," a biting colloquial phrase describing one who is offensively conceited and self-assertive. The door to real wisdom is locked to such a person until a great change takes place in his heart. But this is the day of the clever retort, the witty saying, the speedy quip, but none of these is wisdom. Job's definition stands out in beautiful simplicity. It is a startling, sublime, saving truth: "God understands the way of wisdom, and he knoweth the place thereof. . . . and unto man he saith, Behold, the fear of the Lord, that is wisdom; and to depart from evil is understanding."

The fear of the Lord is not the end of wisdom but the beginning of it. The person who is really wise will fear the Lord. Could the vessel that says to the potter, "I have no need of thee" be wise? Is the creature wise who says to the Creator, "I have no need of thee"? Will the living man dare to ignore the living God and say that is wisdom?

True wisdom starts with God and develops under His direction. Man is never the source of wisdom nor can he develop it, for it can neither begin with nor survive upon a foundation of clay. It must have under it the everlasting arms. Its source is in the eternal, all-wise God.

When Jesus came into this world He said, "I am come to do thy will, O God." That is wisdom. He became a man that He might suffer and feel as we do, for a God of wisdom is sensible to the needs of His creatures. That is why He said to us that if we would save our lives we would lose them, but if we would lose them for His sake we would save them. God is a God of wisdom and has a plan and purpose for every life.

Where then will wisdom be found? In the heart of the man who fears the Lord. This is where it begins and it continues by our finding out what God has planned for us and following after it. Wisdom is finding out how God thinks about things and then acting accordingly. Wisdom is finding out what God has willed for us and seeking to do that will. That is why the Scriptures say of wisdom: "But whoso findeth me findeth life, and shall obtain favour of the Lord. But he that sinneth against me wrongeth his own soul: all they that hate me love death" (Prov. 8:35,36).

Since God has sent His Son into the world saying, "Unto you is born a Saviour," is it wisdom to reject

Him? When the Scriptures tell us to "seek those things which are above" or "walk in the Spirit," is it wisdom to do otherwise? Since Jesus said, "Follow me," and the Word states: "As many as received him to them gave he power to become the sons of God." Is it not wisdom to believe His Word and act upon it? Indeed it is.

When God invites us to come and rest, we who live in this mixed-up generation, is it not wisdom to come to Him for that rest? We are living in a society bored with life and expressing that boredom and frustration in acts of lawlessness and violence. We will never find rest in such ways. Heart rest is found only in Christ.

> "Friends all around me are trying to find
> What the heart yearns for, by sin undermined;
> I have the secret, I know where 'tis found:
> Only true pleasures in Jesus abound."

Two Kinds of Wisdom

There are two kinds of wisdom. One is that natural wisdom with which every man is endowed. It has its roots in itself and rests in itself. It acclaims itself king and will bow to none else. For this reason it is not accepted of God. It is also because of this natural wisdom that the Bible says, "For ye see your calling, brethren, how that not many wise men after the flesh, not many mighty, not many noble, are called: But God hath chosen the foolish things of the world to confound the wise; and God has chosen the weak things of the world to confound the mighty; And base things of the world, and things which are despised, hath God chosen, yea, and things which are not, to bring to nought things that are; THAT NO FLESH SHOULD GLORY IN HIS PRESENCE" (I Cor. 1:26-29).

The other kind of wisdom is true wisdom, a wisdom that is submissive to God. It is the wisdom that wants to do what He wants, and seeks His will. That wisdom is of great value. Concerning it, the Bible says, "Doth not wisdom cry? and understanding put forth her voice?" (Prov. 8:1). Wisdom speaking of itself says, "By me kings reign, and princes decree justice. By me princes rule, and nobles, even all the judges of the earth. I love them that love me; and those that seek me early shall find me. Riches and honour are with me; yea, durable riches and righteousness. My fruit is better than gold, yea, than fine gold; and my revenue than choice silver. I lead in the way of righteousness, in the midst of the paths of judgment: That I may cause those that love me to inherit substance; and I will fill their treasures" (Prov. 8:15-21).

No wonder true wisdom is precious and to be sought after. Out of it comes right judgment, true justice, benevolent rule, and a full heart. These are the very things that we seek but seldom find, because we seek for them in the wrong place.

This same Book of Proverbs goes on to say, "There is that speaketh like the piercings of a sword: but the tongue of the wise is health" (12:18). In other words, just as a sharp sword can cut and injure the body so a sharp tongue cuts a person to the very quick. On the other hand the tongue of the wise brings healing and help. This is why Paul said in Ephesians 4:29, "Let no corrupt communication proceed out of your mouth, but that which is good to the use of edifying, that it may minister grace unto the hearers."

True wisdom is a gift of God to the seeker who searches for it with a humble heart. When the Lord answered Job He said, "Who hath put wisdom in the inward parts? or who hath given understanding to the heart?" (Job 38:36). Job knew the answer just as we know the answer—true wisdom is the work of God.

It was in answer to his humble petition that Solomon received wisdom from God. He had asked for "wisdom and knowledge, that I may go out and come in before this people: for who can judge this thy people, that is so great?" (II Chron. 1:10). The Lord answered, "Wisdom and knowledge is granted unto thee; and I will give thee riches, and wealth, and honour, such as none of the kings have had that have been before thee" (v. 12).

The Queen of Sheba came to see Solomon and to hear his wisdom, "And Solomon told her all her questions: and there was nothing hid from Solomon which he told her not. And when the queen of Sheba had seen the wisdom of Solomon, and the house that he had built, And the meat of his table, and the sitting of his servants, and the attendance of his ministers, and their apparel; his cupbearers also . . . she said to the king, It was a true report which I heard in mine own land of thine acts, and of thy wisdom: Howbeit I believed not their words, until I came, and mine eyes had seen it: and, behold, the one half of the greatness of thy wisdom was not told me: for thou exceedest the fame that I heard" (II Chron. 9:2-6).

David knew the source of true wisdom and that God's purpose for it was that it should pervade every aspect of a human heart. When David's great sins connected with Uriah and Bathsheba were brought home to him, he knew that he had been very unwise so he prayed: "Behold, thou desirest truth in the inward parts: and in the hidden part thou shalt make me to know wisdom" (Ps. 51:6).

Daniel witnessed in his day to the fact that his wisdom was from God. When Nebuchadnezzar's dream was revealed to the prophet in answer to prayer, "Daniel blessed the God of heaven . . . and said, Blessed be the name of God for ever and ever: for wisdom and might are his" (Dan. 2:19,20).

True wisdom causes the simple to make wise decisions. This is the testimony of the Psalmist who said, "The law of the Lord is perfect, converting the soul: the testimony of the Lord is sure, making wise the simple" (Ps. 19:7).

True wisdom causes us to think as we ought to think about God. The inspired apostle wrote, "Let no man deceive himself. If any man among you seemeth to be wise in this world, let him become a fool, that he may be wise. For the wisdom of this world is foolishness with God (this is in respect to spiritual matters such as sin, salvation, God and His ways). For it is written, He taketh the wise in their own craftiness. And again, The Lord knoweth the thoughts of the wise, that they are vain. Therefore let no man glory in men" (I Cor. 3:18-21).

True wisdom causes us to think as we should think about ourselves. This again is a testimony from the Apostle Paul: "For I say, through the grace given unto me, to every man that is among you, not to think of himself more highly than he ought to think; but to think soberly, according as God hath dealt to every man the measure of faith" (Rom. 12:3). What a change this would make in our world! No wonder the Bible says, "When pride cometh, then cometh shame: but with the lowly is wisdom" (Prov. 11:2).

True wisdom causes us to think correctly about our manner of life. The Bible says in this connection: "Who is a wise man and endued with knowledge among you? let him show out of a good conversation (manner of life) his works with meekness of wisdom (that is how a person can prove his wisdom). But if ye have bitter envying and strife in your hearts, glory not, and lie not against the truth. This wisdom (the wisdom that is bitter, full of envy and strife) descendeth not from above, but is earthly, sensual, devilish. For where envying and strife is, there is confusion and every evil work. But the wisdom that is from above is first pure, then peaceable, gentle, and easy to be intreated, full of mercy and good fruits, without partiality, and without hypocrisy. And the fruit of righteousness is sown in peace of them that make peace" (James 3:13-18).

True wisdom will cause us to think rightly about God's purpose for us. "Wherein he hath abounded toward us in all wisdom and prudence: Having made known unto us the mystery of his will, according to his good pleasure which he hath purposed in himself: That in the dispensation of the fulness of times he might gather together in one all things in Christ, both which are in heaven, and which are on earth; even in him: In whom also we have obtained an inheritance, being predestinated according to the purpose of him who worketh all things after the counsel of his own will" (Eph. 1:8-11).

True wisdom will make us think correctly about our time here as well as hereafter. In the 90th Psalm we read: "We spend our years as a tale that is told. The days of our years are threescore years and ten; and if by reason of strength they be fourscore years, yet is their strength labour and sorrow; for it is soon cut off; and we fly away. . . . So teach us to number our days, that we may apply our hearts unto wisdom" (vv. 9-12). Most of us slide along through life, thinking that since we lived yesterday, we will surely live today and tomorrow also. We are deceived into thinking that we have plenty of time to prepare our hearts for meeting God. But true wisdom will have none of this dilatory attitude toward spiritual things. It would have us get right with God now; true wisdom will always keep us ready to meet our Lord.

True wisdom causes us to think the way we ought to think about God's Son. Here is just a sample of what is involved in that: "Christ Jesus . . . is made unto us wisdom, and righteousness, and sanctification, and redemption: that according as it is written, he that glorieth, let him glory in the Lord."

True wisdom always glorifies God. This was the testimony of Paul as he reached the end of that great section of the unveiling of God's unmatched wisdom and mercy in dealing with the Jew. "O the depth of the riches both of the wisdom and knowledge of God! how unsearchable are his judgments, and his ways past finding out! For who hath known the mind of the Lord? or who hath been

111

his counsellor? Or who hath first given to him, and it shall be recompensed unto him again? For of him, and through him, and to him, are all things: to whom be glory for ever. Amen" (Rom. 11:33-36).

What shall we conclude then about wisdom? Learn from Solomon that "the fear of the Lord is the beginning of knowledge: but fools despise wisdom and instruction" (Prov. 1:7).

Job tells us, "And unto man he said, Behold, the fear of the Lord, that is wisdom: and to depart from evil is understanding" (Job 28:28). Right at the beginning of the Psalms we have this admonition: "Be wise now therefore, O ye kings: be instructed, ye judges of the earth. Serve the Lord with fear, and rejoice with trembling. Kiss the Son, lest he be angry, and ye perish from the way, when his wrath is kindled but a little. Blessed are all they that put their trust in him" (Ps. 2:10-12).

Chapter Nine

WHAT SHALL I DO WHEN GOD RISES UP?

There are many questions raised in the Book of Job, but the ones we are considering are chosen for their timeliness and their timelessness. They are the questions of the ages and the important questions of today when men stop long enough to think about the realities of life.

The question now before us is not one to be answered hastily. It certainly is not one we will answer correctly if we are trying to act like very big ducks in very small ponds. If we are going around trying to get others to think we are greater than we really are, we will not have the right answer to this query. This is a question that must be faced when we are alone, faced honestly without any shade of pretense whatever. We need to get off by ourselves where we can stop our games of self-deceit and think seriously about matters that count. This is Job's question: "What then shall I do when God riseth up? and when he visiteth, what shall I answer him?" (Job 31:14).

This is a good question for any person to face at any time. It is not "What shall we do?" but "What shall I do?" In that day when God rises up and we must give an answer to Him personally, we will not be able to hide be-hind each other. We will not be able to pretend that we are part of a group and try to hide behind the faceless-ness of numbers. We will find no escape in saying con-cerning ourselves: "I am no more guilty than a lot of others." There will be no possibility of hedging on our answers. We will have to answer then as we should be answering now, as human beings with lives to live and souls to answer to God for.

In this one query Job faces some facts from which most of us try to hide. The first of these is that God will not be silent forever; and the second is that everyone of us must give an account to God. This is a personal ques-tion to each one of us and calls for a personal answer for such is what God will demand. In that long-ago time, Job knew by revelation that though a man dies he will live again. So if a man considers only this life, he is dan-gerously shortsighted. Things are not always what they seem to be on the surface. There is a day coming when God will rise up and break the silence. He will call each person to give an account before Him and will judge each one in righteousness. One by one we will stand before Him. What will our answer be when there is no escape? when there is no excuse? when the truth must be laid on the line?

We know that when we die our bodies turn back to dust. We seem to grow used to the taste of dust and ashes; that is, we think in terms of this short life only. Our plans are for today; see no farther than the sunset. If we are clothed and have a house over our heads and our stomachs are full, the Scriptures seem to lose their urgent appeal to consider the matters of time and eternity. We are prone to follow those described in Job chapter 21 who, when they think all is going well, ask God to leave them alone. Insurance we want for this life only, as though there was nothing beyond. We act as though the tomorrows would have no shadows and that God would be silent forever.

What we want we want now. Our actions indicate we are afraid that if we die we will somehow be cheated out of our just dues. We want our revenge now. Man's history is a story of torture, evil scheming and plotting man against man. It is the story of rebellion, robbery, aggression and hate which has led to stark terror time after time. Our selfish cry is for rewards now. Like the prodigal son in Luke 15 we want the portion of our heritage now. We want pie in our plates, not pie in the sky. The Holy Spirit through Paul said some very pointed things with regard to the selfish spirit that demands everything at once. "But why dost thou judge thy brother? for we shall all stand before the judgment seat of Christ. For it is written, As I live, saith the Lord, every knee shall bow to me, and every tongue shall confess to God. So then every one of us shall give account of himself to God. Let us not therefore judge one another any more: but judge this rather, that no man put a stumbling-block or an occasion to fall in his brother's way" (Rom. 14:10-13).

Paul is saying to those who want their rewards and revenge now, "Forget it! Live with the fact in mind that you will have to answer to God. Take care of your responsibility to Him and all other things will be right."

The Apostle John, in his first letter, touched on this same subject. He wrote, "He that loveth not his brother abideth in death. Whosoever hateth his brother is a murderer: and ye know that no murderer hath eternal life abiding in him" (I John 3:14,15).

Paul, in writing to the Corinthians, said that there are conditions under which it is better to suffer wrong than to retaliate. There are times when it is better to endure injury and insult than to fight back. So often we want something or we want to do something simply because we claim to have the right to have what is ours. We think God acts too slowly, so we want to get what we think is ours now. This is not a suggestion that we should become milk toasts and let others walk over us. What we are pointing out is that a great many of our problems could be solved quickly, easily and peacefully by asking ourselves two questions. They are the questions Job asked: "What then shall I do when God riseth up? and when he visiteth, what shall I answer him?"

In the light of that day when we stand before God, does it really matter that we have our rewards now? Is it important in the light of that great event that those who have wronged us be put in their place now? Would it not be much better for us to leave our rewards to God? He is the final judge in all of these matters in any case. And as for revenge, we have neither all the facts nor the ability to judge righteous judgment, so why not leave this in God's hands also? Why feed on hate and bitterness when one of these days God will judge the world in righteousness?

We are admonished that in this present life we are to

"let love be without dissimulation. Abhor that which is evil; cleave to that which is good. Be kindly affectioned one to another with brotherly love; in honour preferring one another" (Rom. 12:9,10).

Job knew that his two great questions were related to what he had done in this life. One cannot live to please himself in this world and then pass into the next world scot-free to share all the joys of heaven with all its unbroken bliss forever. There is a reckoning time for the Christian as well as the unbeliever. The believer will have his Christian life evaluated with respect to rewards or loss of rewards. There will be no question concerning his eternal destiny, for that was settled when he trusted in Christ. The judgment of God against sin's guilt and against all else that sin can do against him was fully met when the believer trusted in Jesus Christ as his personal Saviour. The unbeliever, on the other hand, should he leave this life rejecting Christ, will have to face the consequences of the guilt of sin and the consequences of his personal acts of sin.

Job realized that he would have to answer to God for his moral life. This is what he referred to when he said, "I made a covenant with mine eyes; why then should I think upon a maid? For what portion of God is there from above? and what inheritance of the Almighty from on high?" (Job 31:1,2). In plain language Job is saying that he made an agreement with his eyes that he would not look upon a woman with wrong desires in his mind. His questions can then be stated: "For what portion should I have from God above if I were immoral, and what heritage from the Almighty on high?"

In verses 3 and 4 Job says, "Is not destruction to the wicked? and a strange punishment to the workers of iniquity? Doth not he see my ways, and count all my steps?" Here Job by means of questions points out the fact that the wicked will be judged, for God sees all that men do, observing every detail of our conduct. Job realized, what we need to realize, that the answers God will demand of us relate to what is done on earth. This is a personal matter. It is not what others do, but what each of us does that is involved. Job knew that his actions with regard to his servants would be included. If he were stubborn and unkind and uncharitable towards them, this would show up when he appeared before God. Job said, "If I did despise the cause of my manservant or of my maidservant, when they contended with me; What then shall I do when God riseth up? and when he visiteth, what shall I answer him?" (31:13,14).

As with Job so with us. Life is more than passing time, it is building for eternity. We must not make it a time in which we see how much we can get by with, but a time of seeing how much we can store up for the eternal years ahead. It is more than a "this world" affair. In this life we are laying a foundation for the world to come.

If we are to stand before God "unashamed" as John wrote in his first epistle, it is imperative that we find answers to some things that are very real in this life. We must squarely face our sins. This is not a matter we can dodge, for God "sees my ways and counts all my steps." It will do no good to deny our evil actions, because the results are all about us. We shall surely be brought to judgment for our sins sooner or later. This is why we must find the right answer to Job's question: "How can a man be just with God?" We must face God's attitude toward sin and what God has done about it.

The Prophet Ezekiel tells us God's attitude when he says, "The soul that sinneth, it shall die" (Ezek. 18:4).

Paul expresses God's attitude toward sin in these words: "For the wrath of God is revealed from heaven against all ungodliness and unrighteousness of men, who hold the truth in unrighteousness." Paul brings the subject of human sin and guilt to its tragic climax when he says in Romans 3:10-12: "As it is written, There is none righteous, no, not one: There is none that understandeth, there is none that seeketh after God. They are all gone out of the way, they are together become unprofitable; there is none that doeth good, no, not one."

Has God made provision for poor sinners? Is there salvation from such a condition? Is there mercy with God? If so, has He shown it and where can we find it? Is there a way, in spite of what we are, whereby we may be just before God?

God's plan for salvation is possibly best expressed in I Corinthians 15:1-4: "Moreover, brethren, I declare unto you the gospel which I preached unto you, which also ye have received, and wherein ye stand; By which also ye are saved, if ye keep in memory what I preached unto you, unless ye have believed in vain. For I delivered unto you first of all that which I also received, how that Christ died for our sins according to the scriptures;

And that he was buried, and that he rose again the third day according to the scriptures."

You will notice the first thing is that Christ died for our sins. This is in agreement with John 3:16 which tells us that God so loved the world that He gave His only begotten Son to die for us. This is the message of Romans 4:25 which says Christ was delivered for our offenses.

We are next told that He was buried. Would not this be something we would take for granted? No indeed! There had to be assurance that He was dead, for His death was no ordinary death, since He was dying in our place. Joseph of Arimathaea testified to the fact of Christ's death when he wrapped the body for burial and laid it in his own tomb and rolled a great stone across the entrance (Matt. 27:57-60).

The Pharisees were sure He was dead, because they spoke to Pilate concerning Christ's burial. They remembered He had said that after He was dead for three days He would rise again. These men wanted to be sure that the tomb would be protected so that no one could steal Christ's body (Matt. 27:63,64).

Pilate was amazed to learn that Christ was already dead and in order to be sure about it asked the centurian for confirmation. This he readily gave (Mark 15:44). When the soldiers came to break the legs of the persons who had been crucified, they found Christ already dead and so did not break His legs (John 19:32-34).

The third great fact of the gospel is that Christ arose the third day according to the Scriptures. There could be no question about this. He was seen of Cephas, then of the twelve, and then of above 500 brethren at once.

James saw Him and so did all the apostles. Some time later Paul saw Him when he was on the road to Damascus (Acts 9:3-6; I Cor. 15:5-8).

Christ was not only delivered for our offenses but He was raised again on account of our justification (Rom. 4:25). His resurrection was proof that His death on Calvary satisfied the justice of God.

The sentence of death was, and is, upon the human race. Life is our problem. For this reason God sent His Son into the world to die in our place, and He arose again that He might give eternal life to all who place their trust unreservedly in Him. "Therefore as by the offence of one judgment came upon all men to condemnation; even so by the righteousness of one the free gift came upon all men unto justification of life. . . . as sin hath reigned unto death, even so might grace reign through righteousness unto eternal life by Jesus Christ our Lord" (Rom. 5:18,21). It is through faith in Him that we are saved. This is a sure salvation and a present salvation. This is the force of I Corinthians 15:2 and Ephesians 2:8,9. Consequently, when we stand before God the first great question will be with regard to what we did with His remedy for sin, His beloved Son. What will the answer be? Did we receive Him? Did we reject Him? If we received Him, did we go on to neglect Him?

We will have to give an account of the deeds done in the body. Sometime, somewhere as sure as the setting sun, we must answer to God for what we have done in the body. We will then receive as believers either rewards or loss of rewards for those deeds. If unbelievers, then we will suffer stripes of punishment in keeping with the evil we have committed. There is no escape.

As you read these words what are your plans for this day? Are you preparing to take revenge on someone? Are you plotting evil in your heart against someone? Though we might be able to bury such deeds and desires in the depths of the sea we will face the consequences of these things eventually.

If we are to be saved from the penalty of our sins, we must do it now. If we are to receive Christ as Lord we must do it now. It will be too late when we stand before God in judgment. According to Romans 3, every person who stands before God will find the law will leave him speechless. No one will be able to justify his evil deeds when he stands before God.

John surely intimates in his letter that if we have not found the place of "no condemnation in Christ Jesus," our hearts will condemn us. God's holiness will overwhelm us because of our sin.

The whole world has been declared guilty in the sight of God. We will need someone to plead our cause in the face of judgment. This is the ministry of Jesus Christ for all who receive Him. "There is one God, and one mediator between God and men, the man Christ Jesus; Who gave himself a ransom for all, to be testified in due time" (I Tim. 2:5,6). He only is qualified to approach God, for He did no sin, neither was guilt found in His mouth. He alone is qualified to plead our cause, because He died for our offenses and was raised again for our justification.

What will we answer in that day with regard to our

souls? Do we know the Saviour? As to our manner of life, is it lived for God's will or for our own? What are we doing with our gifts? Are we using them for the glory of God? Are we leading our families by our lives and by our teaching in a way that honors God? Will we hear God say to us, "Enter into the joy of the Lord"? Or are we among those to whom He will have to say, "Depart from me, I never knew you"?

Christ will either be our Saviour or our Judge. The choice is ours. This is the day of salvation!